the digital photographer's guide to

PHOTOSHOP
ELEMEN

Improve your photos and create fantastic specia...

LYC 399

the digital photographer's guide to

PHOTOSHOP ELEMENTS

Improve your photos and create fantastic special effects

Barry Beckham

LARK BOOKS
A Division of Sterling Publishing Co., Inc.
New York

The Digital Photographer's Guide to Photoshop Elements:
Improve Your Photographs and Create Fantastic Special Effects

10 9 8 7 6 5 4 3 2 1

Published by Lark Books, a division of
Sterling Publishing Co., Inc.
387 Park Avenue South, New York, N.Y. 10016

Text © The Ilex Press Limited 2004
Images © Barry Beckham, 2004

This book was conceived by ILEX,
The Old Candlemakers, West Street,
Lewes, England, BN7 2NZ.

Distributed in Canada by Sterling Publishing,
c/o Canadian Manda Group, One Atlantic Ave., Suite 105
Toronto, Ontario, Canada M6K 3E7

If you have questions or comments about this book, please contact:
Lark Books
67 Broadway
Asheville, NC 28801
(828) 253-0467

Beckham, Barry, 1950-
      The digital photographer's guide to Photoshop Elements : improve your
   photographs & create fantastic special effects. Barry Beckham-- 1st ed.
      p. cm.
      ISBN 1-57990-528-5 (pbk.)
   1. Photography--Digital techniques. 2. Photography--Special effects
   3. Adobe Photoshop elements. II. Title.

TR267.C66 2004

778.3--dc21

                                          2004007919

Printed in Hong Kong

contents

Part four

4 Creative digital imaging   108

Part five

5 Real world projects   186

Part six

6 Reference   206

Introduction

Photoshop Elements gives you complete control over color. Take a shot in color, then turn it into black and white. Then use the tools at your command to adjust every tonal level, and every aspect of brightness and contrast. You can give a new photo a vintage look, or take an old photo and make it look like it was shot five minutes ago. With a little technique, almost anything is possible.

The Digital Way

Digital photography has become a fascinating hobby for many people since the digital revolution first began. Since then, the rollercoaster of technological advancements has never slowed down.

The constant upgrade of cameras and equipment with ever-higher pixel counts and the improvements in film and flatbed scanner resolution have all been great news for photographers and for the quality of our pictures. On the other hand, the never-ending improvements and updates make people justifiably nervous of spending their hard-earned money on the latest equipment because of the worry that it may go out of date very quickly.

I would suggest, however, that you do not concern yourself too much with the endless chase of pixels and resolution. There really isn't a need to replace your equipment constantly as the technology moves on—as long as it still works.

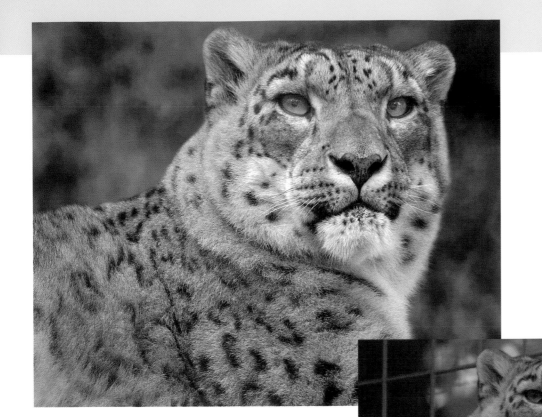

The prints I make at 20 by 16 inches are considered good quality images by some very discerning professional and amateur photographers. Most of these prints are taken from images shot with a midrange 3 megapixel camera; so, while it might be nice to own a top-of-the-range 6 megapixel camera, it is certainly not essential. You can use and enjoy your equipment no matter what the pixel count or resolution.

This book is concerned with making pictures better. This could involve small changes in color; the removal of objects that spoil your images; or the correction of some of the common faults that are difficult to avoid. I will also show you how to take your photographs further, whether they are shot using a digital camera or scanned with a flatbed or negative scanner.

Photoshop Elements 2, produced by the Adobe Corporation, is now in its second version. Adobe produces Photoshop 7, a powerful, complex, and expensive program that is recognized as the world-standard software for image editors and professionals. Realizing that Photoshop 7 was out of reach for many people, Adobe designed Elements 2 specifically for amateur photographers and hobbyists—although businesses use it too.

Removing this big cat from its cage is a cinch in Photoshop Elements. You can select any part of an image and move or remove it, change a background, transform the focus of a shot, and blur and sharpen at will. Here, the background has been changed and blurred, getting rid of the cage mesh. Also, the colors and tones of the shot have been adjusted and the image has been cropped to enhance the composition.

Introduction continued

Photoshop Elements can create complex montages, where images or parts of images are layered and blended together to create stunning new composite shots. You have complete control over how the different elements interract with each other. See how three simple photos—fishing boats in a harbor, a seagull, and distressed wooden slats—build into one dynamic whole. This is only a basic example of what Photoshop Elements can do.

Adobe removed many of the complex parts of Photoshop 7 that amateurs would never use and replaced them with more convenient tools to allow us to learn quickly and carry out the tasks we want more easily. Because it is a fraction of the cost of Photoshop 7, it would be easy to assume that Elements is lacking somewhere. Flick through the pages of this book, however, and you will soon see that the program provides you with all the tools you need to improve your images.

Elements is a powerful image-editing tool. Apart from using it to make corrections to pictures to improve them, for example, you can create new images from scratch by combining two or more images in a montage. You can also use the tools of Photoshop Elements to bring out your creative side by adding filter and artistic effects to your pictures.

One word of warning: both digital photography and Photoshop Elements can be highly addictive pastimes, and it may be three weeks before you leave your computer after starting to read this book. It is a fascinating hobby, and you need just a little learning to get the best from it. So, stock your fridge and join us on this digital journey of discovery.

Photoshop Elements has inherited Photoshop's vast range of effects filters. Using these, you can recreate the effects of natural artistic media such as oil paint, watercolors, or charcoal, add artificial lighting to a scene, add strange new colors or textures, and much, much more. Filters can be combined and faded on demand, and thanks to Elements instant Undo, *you are free to experiment to your heart's content.*

getting started

This book is not intended as a technical manual. Instead, it introduces you to the tools and processes of Photoshop Elements through practical examples and tutorials. By following these, you can learn tricks and techniques that you can apply to your own images to get great results. Photoshop Elements prides itself on its ease of use, but there are still some things you should know before you delve any deeper into its tools and features. This section outlines the basics: the core concepts of digital images, how to get them from your camera and into Elements, and how to use the program's interface. Read on and you will know everything you need to start creating great pictures of your own.

Importing Images from a Digital Camera

There are many digital cameras on the market, and many ways in which they store images. Generally, they connect to your computer using a standard USB connection, using the cable supplied by the manufacturer. You should have no trouble downloading your images in this way, but you should always check and follow the instructions given with your equipment; in some cases, you may need to install some software from the camera manufacturer to enable the download process to work.

Downloading images directly from your camera is fine, but it may mean using up battery power. To avoid that, you will need to hook up your camera to an electrical outlet. Another popular way to the same end is via a card reader: an inexpensive device that attaches to your computer via a USB connection. Card readers can be purchased that read any type of storage card, or even several types.

Once connected, you simply remove your storage card from the camera and place it in the slot on the card reader. Your images can then be downloaded easily—Windows or Mac OS will treat the storage card as it would a CD-ROM or any other storage device. Battery power is not required. Windows XP users will find that the operating system recognizes the storage card as it is placed into the card reader, notices that the card is packed with digital images, then asks what it should do with the files.

Resolution—pixels, megapixels, and ppi

Throughout this book we will be referring to pixels and resolution. These are important for one reason: when you are working on an image in Elements, it makes little difference whether you are working on an image from a 2 megapixel camera or a 6 megapixel camera. When it comes to printing it out, however, size really does matter.

The smallest unit of a digital image is the pixel: one square dot with its own color and brightness values. Any image has a physical size measured in pixels—e.g. 1600 x 1200, or 1600 pixels wide by 1200 pixels high. In digital photography, we need to qualify that by saying how many of those pixels are visible in an inch of paper or screen surface. Computer monitors are designed to display images at a resolution of either 72 or 96 pixels per inch (ppi), but a printed image is less forgiving. When we print out a photo, we want the image to print out at a resolution of 300ppi for true photo quality, or at least 150ppi for a convincing effect.

TIP

Check that the software supplied with your camera is suitable for your operating system, i.e. Windows 98, Windows ME, Windows XP. If not, you may find that an up-to-date version of the software needed will be available on the camera manufacturer's website.

The average 2 megapixel digital camera can create an image of 1600 x 1200 pixels in high-quality mode. If we printed this out at 300ppi the print would be 5.33 inches wide by 4 inches high, and while we could print it larger there would be some drop in quality. The average 5 megapixel camera gives you more options: it can create an image large enough to print out at 8.54 inches wide by 6.4 inches high at 300ppi. Basically, a higher resolution image can be printed out at larger sizes without losing definition or gaining a jagged appearance. Alternatively, you can crop in on part of an image and blow it up, then still get a good-looking printed result.

❮ *A storage card reader gives you quick and easy access to your digital photographs. As well as saving you from having to plug your camera into your computer, it also doesn't waste your camera's battery. Storage card readers are available for every card format, and some can cope with more than one: this model can read CompactFlash, SmartMedia, MultiMedia Card, and SD Memory Card formats.*

> For this shot, taken with a 3 megapixel camera, the original 8.9Mb file would fit a space 30 inches by 20 inches at a resolution of 72ppi. If printed at 300ppi it would cover approximately 7 by 5 inches. Had the same image been taken by a camera with a lower pixel count, the resolution, and therefore the quality of the image, could be retained, but the size on screen would be reduced to 15 by 10 inches. If printed at 7 x 5 inches, the resolution would drop to 150ppi and quality would be reduced.

Why does resolution matter?

If you're confused by resolution, think about the images used in billboard advertisements. We see them everywhere —large, colorful, dynamic, and apparently sharp. Walk up close to the billboard, however, and you will see that they are not so sharp—in fact, the images are made up of lots of dots.

Let's assume that the billboard we are looking at is 20 feet by 10 feet and that 6 million dots have been used to create that dynamic poster. What would happen if we removed 3 million of those dots? The poster would lose quality, because fewer dots would be spread across that 20 by 10 foot area. To retain the same quality, we would have to reduce the size of the hoarding so that the remaining 3 million pixels continued to give us the same sharp image.

The same principle works when you print out digital photos. Both a 4 megapixel camera and a 2 megapixel camera can take an image which you could print out at 8 by 10 inches. The difference is that the 4 megapixel shot would contain enough information to print out at a resolution of 240ppi—which would be good photo quality if we consider 300dpi as the ideal. The 2 megapixel shot only contains enough information to print out at 150ppi. It will still look acceptable, but the shot will not have the same level of fine detail or definition.

Importing Images from a Scanner

Just a few years ago, the only practical method for getting images onto the computer was via a flatbed scanner. They were large and expensive, but did an excellent job. These days they can be bought for very reasonable prices. and have evolved to a state where high-quality results are obtainable from a compact desktop model.

A flatbed scanner is a welcome addition to the digital photographer's armory. It will not be long before family and friends discover your digital skills and you are asked to restore an old family photograph or remove some intrusive object from a valued picture.

Many of the scanners now available come with a film-scanning hood that allows negatives and slides to be scanned as well as prints. If you have yet to purchase a flatbed scanner and you have negatives to scan, this is something worth considering. Of course, dedicated slide and negative scanners are also available.

When you use your scanner you will see that you have several choices to make about scanning resolution. These can be a bit baffling, especially when you compare the 72ppi resolution images that you see from your digital camera to the choices you have in your scanning software, where 2700ppi and higher settings are available.

These very high resolutions exist so that you can scan small images such as a postage stamp or a color slide or negative and still get a decent-sized print from the original scan. As you increase the size of the image using Photoshop Elements, the dots that make up the resolution have to stretch over a wider area. However, if the scan resolution is high to start with, you can get away with enlarging the image without any great loss of quality.

If you are scanning a Letter-sized photograph and choose a resolution of 2700ppi, the resulting file size will be enormous. If you are intending to make a bigger print than Letter-size from a Letter-sized scan, that may be the option you choose, but your computer would need the power to handle the file sizes. For a Letter-sized finished print from a Letter-sized scan, it is unlikely that you would need a scanning resolution of anything greater than 300ppi. So, for small objects, push

❮ *A good A4 flatbed scanner, such as this Epson Perfection 2400 Photo, is a wise investment for the digital photographer with a backlog of 35mm negatives and prints. With a 2400dpi optical resolution and a built in transparency adaptor, it can cope with prints and slides.*

up the resolution and for larger ones reduce it.

If in doubt, it is far better to scan at a higher resolution than you need and reduce the file size later using the *Image Size* palette in Elements.

This same advice is also valid for film and negative scanners. Due to the small size of a negative or slide, scanning resolutions of 2700ppi become useful as they enable you to print at Letter size or larger.

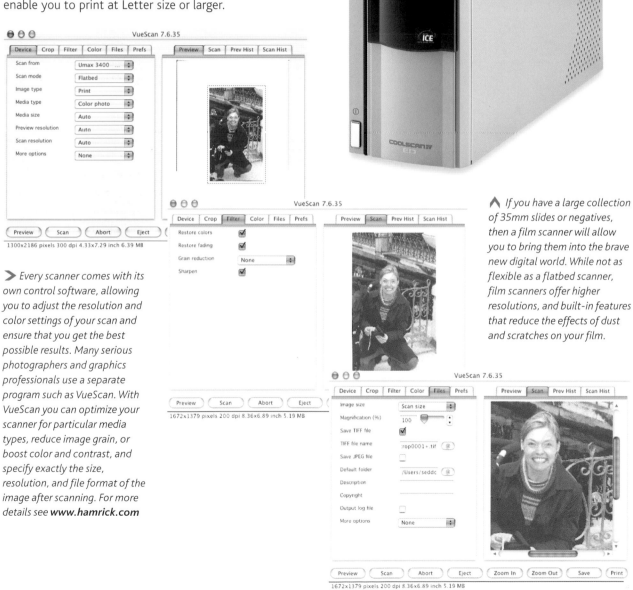

➤ Every scanner comes with its own control software, allowing you to adjust the resolution and color settings of your scan and ensure that you get the best possible results. Many serious photographers and graphics professionals use a separate program such as VueScan. With VueScan you can optimize your scanner for particular media types, reduce image grain, or boost color and contrast, and specify exactly the size, resolution, and file format of the image after scanning. For more details see **www.hamrick.com**

▲ If you have a large collection of 35mm slides or negatives, then a film scanner will allow you to bring them into the brave new digital world. While not as flexible as a flatbed scanner, film scanners offer higher resolutions, and built-in features that reduce the effects of dust and scratches on your film.

Scanning Real Objects

Flatbed scanners are not only good for scanning flat subjects like a photograph or pages of a book; they can also scan real objects, such as the sea urchin shown below.

When you are scanning real objects, you need to select something that does not have too much depth and lay it carefully onto the flatbed glass. This sea urchin was about one inch in diameter. Be careful not to scratch the glass surface of your flatbed scanner, or this single scan could work out to be very expensive. You can close the lid of the scanner on the subject, but obviously it will not fully close on a solid object. Close the flatbed lid carefully as far as it will go. There might be some light spillage around the edges of the scanned subject, which shows up as a colored halo around the image. However, you are likely to be scanning the object for use in another picture for which the background is going to be removed anyway.

Alternatively, rather than closing the flatbed lid onto your object, try to find some black cloth or other material to lay over the subject during the scan.

Use the same resolution choices as described on pages 14–15. If the subject is small, use a higher scanning resolution; if it is big, reduce the scanning resolution. Whatever resolution you use, the file sizes should not be so big that your computer has difficulty handling them.

◄ Great images can be produced in Elements without using a camera at all. You can scan flowers directly on flatbed scanners, but be careful to avoid crushing them with the scanner lid or the cloth you lay over them.

➤ Almost anything can be scanned, including pencils or paintbrushes. You may want to use these objects for importing into other images.

Importing Frames from Video

If you have a digital video camera, you can also incorporate still frames from your movies into your Photoshop Elements work. While you can't expect the same resolution or detail that you would get from a standard digital camera, it is another source of imagery to use. Elements has its own tool to help you import this material.

1 You need to import your video onto the PCX. To do this, refer to your camera manufacturer's instructions. Once you have a sample of your video footage imported onto your PC, go to the *Menu Bar* and select *File > Import > **Frame From Video**.

Click the *Browse* button, locate the video footage on the PC and double-click the file name. Your video will appear in the *Frame From Video* palette.

2 You can use the standard video controls to play back the video clip or you can use the slider bar to find the frame you want to grab quickly. Pause the video, hit the *Grab Frame* button, and the grabbed frame will appear in a separate window. You can then save that file to your hard disk.

Be aware that the quality of these images will vary between different video cameras due to the file sizes they record.

It is not necessary to stop the video while grabbing a frame. If you require a series of grabbed frames from a moving video, continue to click the *Grab Frame* button as the video runs. Elements will grab as many frames as you wish.

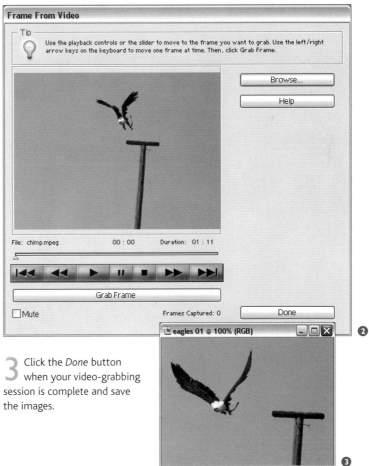

3 Click the *Done* button when your video-grabbing session is complete and save the images.

work area

TOOLBAR

SELECTION TOOLS

MENU BAR

SHORTCUT BAR

OPTIONS BAR

The Elements Work Area

Let's look at the Elements work area in a little more detail. Most parts of the Elements interface can be set to "float" anywhere on screen, but by default you should find the *Toolbar* on the left, the *Options*, *Shortcut*, and *Menu* bars at the top of the screen, and the *Palette Well* on the right. For the moment, we'll just cover where to find the tools and various options. We'll cover what they do and how you use them, as we go further into the book.

The Toolbar

The Toolbar *houses the three types of tools that are available. The functional tools are used to manipulate and change images. They include the* Crop *tool, for cropping pictures to the size and shape you want;* Painting *tools to add pixels, effects, and other changes; the* Type *tool; and various* Shape *tools.*

Other tools do not change images in themselves, but are used in conjunction with others to make changes. The selection tools fall into this category; you use them to prepare the way for another, more functional, tool. The selection tools are some of the most important groups of tools on the Toolbar.

Photoshop Elements offers many different tools to make selections, which indicates their importance to digital photography. If you want to edit a particular part of an image without affecting other areas of an image, you make a selection of that part first. The edge of the selection looks like a moving dotted line and is often referred to as "marching ants."

There are also some tools that just affect the environment you are working in. These include tools such as the Move *tool, the* Hand *tool, the* Zoom *tool, and the* Eye Dropper *tool.*

As you look at the Toolbar, *you will see that some tools have a small black triangle icon in the bottom right corner of the main icon. Click and hold on this icon and other options will roll out for you to select from.*

Individual tools will be explained as they arise in the tutorials throughout this book, but let's jump to the bottom of the Toolbar *to look at the* Color Picker. *You can select the foreground color by clicking the foreground square and the background by clicking the background square.*

The Color Picker *palette that opens up when you click either square allows you to select any color or shade of color and transfer that to the* Color Picker *on the* Toolbar.

MARQUEE TOOLS — MOVE TOOL
LASSOS — MAGIC WAND
SELECTION BRUSH — GRADIENT TOOL
SHAPE TOOLS — TYPE TOOLS
PAINT BUCKET — CROP TOOL
PAINTBRUSH — PENCIL
ERASERS — RED EYE BRUSH
BLUR — SHARPEN
SPONGE TOOL — SMUDGE TOOL
DODGE — BURN
CLONE — EYE DROPPER
HAND — ZOOM
SWITCH FG/BG COLORS
SELECT FOREGROUND COLOR
SELECT BACKGROUND COLOR
DEFAULT FG/BD COLORS

CLICK AND HOLD ON THE BLACK TRIANGLE ICON TO SEE OTHER VARIATIONS ON THE BASIC TOOL

Rectangular Marquee Tool   M
Elliptical Marquee Tool   M

MARCHING ANTS

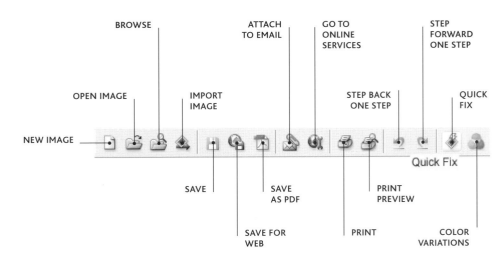

BROWSE

OPEN IMAGE

NEW IMAGE

IMPORT
IMAGE

ATTACH
TO EMAIL

GO TO
ONLINE
SERVICES

STEP
FORWARD
ONE STEP

STEP BACK
ONE STEP

QUICK
FIX

SAVE

SAVE FOR
WEB

SAVE
AS PDF

PRINT

PRINT
PREVIEW

COLOR
VARIATIONS

Quick Fix

The Menu Bar

The Menu Bar *at the very top of the screen is now pretty standard and much the same as many other software packages. You will get details of where and how to access these areas and tools as you proceed through the tutorials.*

The Shortcut Bar

The Shortcut Bar *is also a standard feature in modern software such as word processors, spreadsheets, and paint packages. If you hold the cursor over any of the* Shortcut *icons, the name of the tool will be displayed as a* Tool Tip, *which is a reminder of what the shortcut links to.*

The Options Bar

The Toolbar *options will change to reflect any tool you select from the* Toolbar. *It is worth taking a look at some of the options that appear in the* Options Bar *as you select a tool.*

That said, in a lot of manipulations, the default settings of many tools work pretty well. So, if in doubt, try the default setting first before making any alterations.

This is the Options Bar *for the* Marquee *tool. As you might expect, the options on the bar differ wildly from tool to tool, so hover over the button and use* Tool Tips *to work out anything you don't understand.*

The Elements environment will soon become familiar to you as you work through the tutorials and processes covered in the later chapters of this book. Bear in mind that the Photoshop Elements interface is very similar in most respects to the professional version of Photoshop. Should you ever move up to Photoshop 7 you will not have to learn from scratch.

RECTANGULAR
MARQUEE

ELLIPTICAL
MARQUEE

SET FEATHER
SIZE

CHOOSE NORMAL OR
FIXED MARQUEE

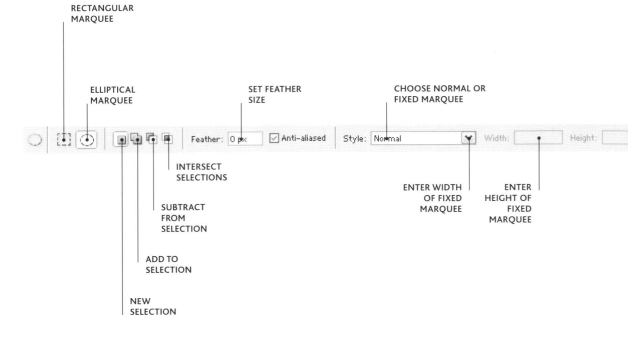

INTERSECT
SELECTIONS

SUBTRACT
FROM
SELECTION

ADD TO
SELECTION

NEW
SELECTION

ENTER WIDTH
OF FIXED
MARQUEE

ENTER
HEIGHT OF
FIXED
MARQUEE

The Elements Work Area continued

| Layer Styles | How To | Filters | Effects | Swatches | Undo History | Navigator | Info | Hints | Layers |

| Layer Sty | How | Filt | Effects | tches | History | gator | rs |

The Palette Well

The Palette Well, found along the top right of the screen, can have a different appearance on different monitors. This depends on what screen resolution your monitor is running at. The most common screen resolution is 1024 by 768 pixels, although working at a higher resolution is recommended if your monitor will allow it.

Elements places so much into the Palette Well that the tabs may be shown overlapped if you are running at 1024 by 768 resolution. However, as you move the cursor over each tab, they are revealed to make selection easier. At higher resolutions, the Palette Well should be more spread out.

Click and drag the tabs in the Palette Well and you can drag any of the palettes out onto your desktop, which can be useful if you need to access one often as you work. Click the small red cross at the top right of the palette and they snap back into the Palette Well.

You will be directed to the relevant palettes as they are explained in the book. It is worth looking at the Browser tab located in the Palette Well as this will give you a visual route to selecting your images.

If the Browser tab is not in your Palette Well, you can select it from the Menu Bar via Window > **File Browser**. To locate it in your Palette Well, click the black triangle icon on the top right indicated by the word More and choose Dock to Palette Well.

The file browser will show each of your images as a thumbnail; double-clicking the thumbnail will open the file into Elements. A single click will highlight the thumbnail, showing you a bigger version in the viewing panel bottom left.

If your images were taken with a digital camera, the technical details will appear in the extreme bottom-left panel. This is a great help if you need reminding of what settings you used for a particular shot.

Undo History

Another palette from the Palette Well that we will need from time to time is the Undo History palette. If we open an image on screen and click the Undo History, we will see that the palette has already recorded the Open command.

As we carry out each task such as cropping and cloning, each stage will be recorded in the Undo History. It records the last 20 commands by default, but we can adjust that upwards or downwards in Preferences. If we make an error while carrying out our manipulations we can jump back to any of these 20 stages using this palette.

The Undo History palette can be dragged out or dropped back in the Palette Well just like any other palette.

The Layers palette

One of the most important tabs in the Palette Well *and one that we will visit often is the* Layers *palette. Click the* Layers *tab and the palette will roll down from its holding position. We can also click the* Layers *tab and drag the palette out onto our desktop if that is more convenient. To replace it just click and drag the tab back into the* Palette Well *or tick the* Close Palette to Palette Well *option via the* More *button. Hit the red cross and the palette will return to the* Palette Well.

What are layers? Think of them as sheets of clear plastic that you can lay over your photo. You can copy parts of the photo, or another photo, to one of those sheets and move them around. Alternatively, imagine that you could use one of those sheets as a filter, to improve the contrast or adjust the brightness of all or part of your image. Best of all, if you make a change to your image on one of those sheets, and regret the change

later on, you can just get rid of the sheet and go back to the image as it was.

In fact, layers are a little more complicated than that. Layers have options for Opacity, *so that you can make any changes made on the layer or any picture elements on it more or less transparent. You can also use the* Blend Mode *option to change how the layer interacts with those below it. We'll demonstrate some useful tricks using* Opacity *and blend modes later on in the book.*

The Layers *palette will show a thumbnail of the image we have on screen. You might also see a small padlock to the right, which indicates whether the layer is locked—the background layer will be by default. While a layer is locked, some options, such as making the layer transparent, are not available. To remove the lock on the background layer, double click the thumbnail and type a new name in the* New Layer *dialog that appears.*

We can have as many layers as we can cope with and each layer can be dragged up or down the stack. This may be important to ensure we have one object behind another to achieve a certain effect in the final image.

To the left of the thumbnail we have a small paintbrush symbol that tells us which layer we have selected for editing, and to the left of that there is a small eye that allows us to turn off the layer so that it temporarily becomes invisible on screen.

At the top left of the palette you will find a drop-down menu with a number of blend modes. These affect how a layer interacts with the layers below it. We will see how this becomes useful in many of the tutorials later on in the book.

All the options we find by clicking the More *button, we will also find duplicated in the layers section of the* Menu Bar.

The three icons located at the bottom of the Layers *palette include the* Trashcan *where we can drag and drop unwanted layers, the* Create New Layer *icon, and the* Create Adjustment Layer *icon.*

TIP

An adjustment layer is a special form of layer that you'll find invaluable the more you work with Elements. These enable you to make adjustments to the brightness, contrast, color, or tone of an image, but the changes are actually made to a separate layer—the adjustment layer—and not the image itself. The main advantage is that you can toggle the visibility of the adjustment layer if you're not sure about its effects later on, or even dump it altogether. As you haven't changed a single pixel of the image, it will still be intact underneath.

This section covers how to put right some of the more common faults in images using simple changes via Elements *Quick Fix* options. Although you can spend hours creating all sorts of way-out and creative images using Photoshop Elements, you still need to make certain adjustments to the pictures beforehand. Many of those changes are pretty standard, and you will find that you constantly revisit the more common tools. Photoshop Elements groups most of these tools together in one place, under the *Quick Fix* palette. Some of these tools create subtle changes, others bring about more dramatic effects.

making your photographs
look good

Quick Fix Tools

Usually in life we can have little faith in those who offer us a quick fix, such as curing baldness with a miracle lotion, or losing weight as you sleep with a wonder cure. However, Elements' *Quick Fix* options might restore your optimism: this is one quick fix that actually works!

No matter how you get your images onto the computer, there are almost always some slight corrections you will need to make to your pictures, usually affecting the color or tonal values, increasing the sharpness, or rotating, or flipping the image. This is true of scanned images as well as images from digital cameras. The *Quick Fix* tool in Photoshop Elements allow you to address those faults quickly and easily from just one palette. Some of these options are demonstrated in the next few tutorials.

What makes an image appealing apart from its subject matter is the tonal range of the image, the contrast, and the color balance. Elements' *Quick Fix* palette allows us to address all of these from one place.

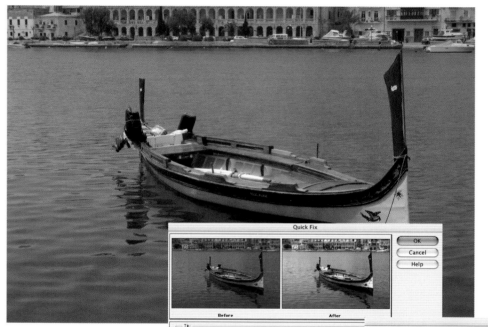

Elements brings up all your choices for a quick fix in one handy palette and shows you a before and after thumbnail before you commit to any changes. From the Quick Fix *panel click* Brightness > **Auto Contrast** *and then the* Apply *button; the* After *thumbnail reflects the changes about to be made. The result can be slight or significant, depending on the tonal range of your original image. If the tonal range is already good, Elements has little to fix. However, you often don't appreciate how flat the tonal range of an image is until you have the "before" and "after" images to compare.*

This example image shows a fairly pleasant vacation shot, but one that lacks that certain sparkle. It can be improved with Quick Fix *tools.*

The Quick Fix *tools can be found in the* Menu Bar *via* Enhance > **Quick Fix** *or by clicking the icon from the* Shortcut *bar, which is much quicker.*

Click the OK *button if you want to commit the quick fix to the image and evaluate the change. If you change your mind afterwards, select the* Undo History *tab from the* Palette Well *and click back one stage.*

If you click Brightness > **Auto Levels** *and then the* Apply *button, the thumbnail will reflect the changes about to be made. You can see from the example image that applying* Levels *has created a much bluer and more cool-looking image, especially when compared to the warm tones of the* Auto Contrast *option.*

Click Color Correction > **Auto Color** *and* Apply *and you will see that the color has been subtly changed to create a better, more lifelike result.*

If you want to make a few manual changes to your color, select Color Correction > **Hue and Saturation**. *From the slider controls adjust the* Hue, Saturation, *or* Lightness. *Probably the most common choice here would be to increase or decrease* Saturation.

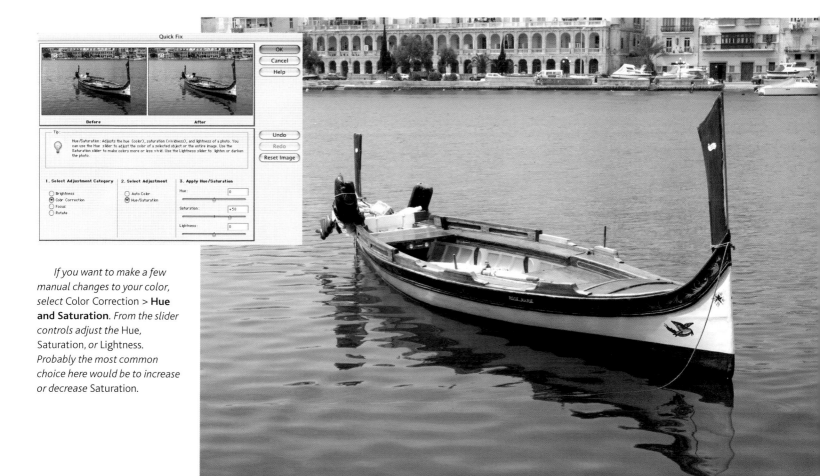

Quick Fix Tools continued

The Quick Fix *option also allows you to sharpen an image. To see the effect of this sharpening, you should first enlarge your image using the* Zoom *tool from the* Toolbar. *Select* Quick Fix *and apply the* Focus > **Auto Focus** *command, and you will see the subtle changes that Elements makes.*

The Quick Fix *palette also allows you to rotate and flip images easily. In some cases, this can make quite a difference to your images. In this example, I decided I preferred to have the pelican swimming right to left rather than left to right.*

I selected the Quick Fix *shortcut* Rotate > **Flip Horizontal** *and clicked the* Apply *and* OK *buttons. This simple change of composition gives the image more appeal than the original.*

The other flip option, Rotate
> **Flip Vertical** *could be used to
flip a reflection image that was
originally shot in water.*

*When you shoot digital
images in portrait mode they
often appear on their side when
you first see them opened on
screen. Using the* Quick Fix
option, then Rotate > **Rotate
90 Left** *will put them right.*

Cropping

Why do you need to crop your images at all? Usually, you will be cropping either to remove unwanted detail, such as a person half in and half out of the frame, or to create a better composition than was possible to achieve when the photograph was taken.

Cropping to improve a composition

1 This is a good example of an image that can be improved with a crop. We do not need all the detail above and below the rower and it can be safely removed.

2 As you select the *Crop* tool from the *Toolbar*, a number of options appear at the top of the screen. If you are just doing a basic crop you can ignore them completely.

3 Drag out the crop shape onto the picture space and don't worry about getting the crop selection right first time. Elements shields the area to be cropped to enable you to evaluate your crop more easily.

4 You can left-click and drag any of the toggles that appear around the edge of the bounding box and drag out the shape and adjust it till you get it just right. Once you have your crop selected, you can complete the task by hitting the *Enter* key, by clicking the tick on the top right of the *Options Bar* or by selecting another tool from the *Toolbar*.

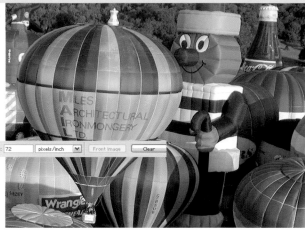

You can also crop to a target size and resolution. This is useful, for example, when preparing several images of the same size for a website.

In this example, the image size started out at 10 by 8 inches at 200ppi. If you want an 8 by 6 inch image at 72ppi, you can input that size onto the Options Bar after selecting the Crop tool.

You can drag out a shape that selects almost the entire image or just a small part of it. Whatever portion you select, the resulting image would still be 8 by 6 inches at 72ppi. In the example above, I selected just a small part of the image from the top right corner of the shot and Elements resized it to fit.

It is best to avoid increasing size or resolution from the original image if you can avoid it. While Elements would carry out this task, it can only increase the resolution by interpolating pixels. What you gain in size from the process, you will lose in definition and detail. As a rule of thumb, an image can be reduced in quality for e-mail or web use, but a low-quality image should not be increased in size to create a much bigger print.

Creative cropping

Cropping and rotating can be used creatively to improve a picture. This image has some impact already, but the vulture sits too square in the space to make it a dynamic shot.

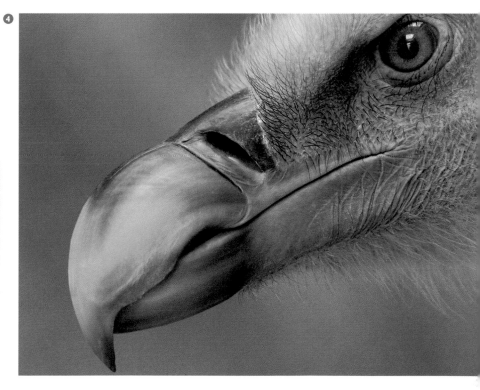

2 Select the *Crop* tool from the *Toolbar* and drag out a crop shape over the bird's head. If you move the cursor outside of the bounding box it changes to linked arrows.

3 Elements is telling you that with a click and drag you can now rotate the crop shape. Rotate the crop until the eye is up near the top right corner of the square crop shape and the beak points down to the bottom left corner.

4 Don't worry if you have to crop slightly outside of your image at the corners—you can always repair those with the *Clone* tool later. With the cursor inside the bounding box, you can also click and drag the whole shape, so this one tool allows you to perform the whole procedure.

Sloping Horizons

When you use a flatbed scanner to scan an image it can be difficult to get the image completely straight on the flatbed glass. This means that the resulting scan will not be straight. Similarly, it's just as easy to take skewed shots with a digital camera as it is with an traditional 35mm SLR. Elements can fix it, either way.

Photoshop Elements has a command that not only straightens the image, but crops away the unwanted white areas around the outside of the scan. From the Menu Bar, *select* Image > Rotate > **Straighten and Crop Image** *and Elements does the rest for you*

Rotating the horizon

1 A sloping horizon is often the result of not holding the camera level at the shooting stage. To correct a sloping horizon, you can use a grid as a guide to ensure that the horizon ends up straight.

2 From the *Menu Bar*, select View > **Grid** and Elements will apply a grid to the image. If you are working on a 3 megapixel image, as was the case here, the gridlines will be quite close together, cluttering the image. You can go to *Edit > Preferences* > **Grid** and change the settings to space them out.

3 Increase the gridline setting so that the spacing is much easier to see and from the drop-down menu select a bright color such as yellow. From the *Menu Bar* select *Image > Rotate > **Custom*** and you can type in an angle, rotating the image by any degree either right or left. I found that about 1.7 degrees was perfect for this image.

This process straightens the horizon, but you then need to crop away the corners that have been exposed during the turning process.

Transforming the horizon

1 Here is an alternative method of straightening the horizon. Select *Image > Transform > **Free Transform***. If you are working on the background layer, Photoshop Elements realizes that what you are asking is not yet possible. To rotate your image with the *Transform* tools, you must first convert the background image into a layer. You can do that manually, but the software is coming to your aid here, and displays a message for us.

2 Allow Elements to assist you and click *OK* and *OK* again from the *New Layer* box. Elements has now placed a bounding box around the entire image. If you move your pointer outside of this box beyond the edge of the image, it will change to a linked arrow.

3 Click and drag to rotate the image and level up the horizon. This option does exactly the same job as the first, but you can now deal with those corners at the same time and in a slightly different way.
Hold down the Shift key and move your pointer to a corner toggle. Drag out the toggles of each corner so that the image fills the spaces left by the rotation. Hit *Enter* or click the tick box on the *Options Bar* to complete the transformation.

4 Because you have previously changed your image from the default background to a layer, you should select *Flatten* from the *Layers* menu before saving. You also need to go to *View > **Grid*** and the grid will be removed and the job completed. This process is fine for small changes, but any larger transformations that increase your images should be avoided.

Adjusting Contrast

When you make adjustments to an image via the *Levels* command, it may greatly improve the foreground, but be far too much for the sky, which becomes pale and lacking in detail. You may feel caught between a rock and a hard place: if you get one part of the image right, another part will look worse. One solution is to make a selection of each part and manipulate each one separately using different settings. Another way, which allows you more flexibility, is to use the *Adjustment Layer* tools.

1 If you look at the example, above, you can see an image in need of adjustment via the *Levels* command. Rather than use the auto settings in *Quick Fix*, you can take a more hands-on approach by clicking the *Layers* tab from the *Palette Well*. You can then click the *Adjustment Layer* icon at the bottom left of the *Layers* palette and select *Levels* from the options that appear.

2 You can adjust the levels in the image using the slider controls in the *Levels* palette. The slider on the right controls the lighter tones in the image; the one on the left darker tones; and the middle one the midtones. You can adjust the tones manually using the sliders with the RGB channel selected, or you can select the color channels separately from the drop-down menu, then adjust the levels for each one. The last method can be more effective if, for example, you wish to retain the warm tones of a sunset.

3 Another way to adjust the tones in subjects like this, where the snow has caused a blue cast, is to click the *Eye Dropper* tool on the right of the *Levels* palette. Look carefully at the image and click down again within the picture space somewhere on the snow. The place you choose should be the lightest tone you can find that retains detail. You can do the same with the other *Eye Dropper* icons and click in the darkest tone with detail or a midtone, but the lighter tone options seem to work better.

Get this selection right and the image will be transformed; click *OK* if the result looks right. If it doesn't, hold down the Alt key and the *Cancel* button will change to a *Reset* button; you can then choose another place to select from. Click the *Layers* tab from the *Palette Well* to see your adjustment layer.

You will also see that your manipulations have destroyed all the detail in the sky in this example, but all is not lost. This is where the adjustment layer comes into play.

4 Select the *Brush* tool from the *Toolbar,* then go to the *Options Bar* and select a soft-edged brush of approximately 100 pixels diameter and an *Opacity* of 100%.

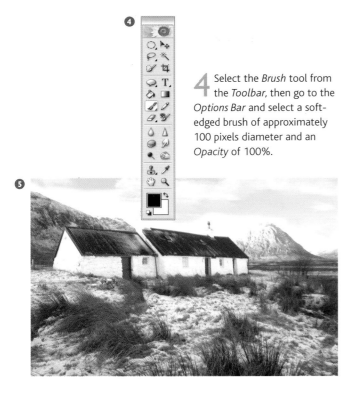

5 Select black as the foreground color from the *Color Picker* and spray along the top edge of the sky. You will see that you are able to bring back the depth of tone from the original sky. This is because the adjustment layer has not permanently changed any of the pixels in the image. The adjustment layer allows you to mask the sky selectively to reveal the original tones.

6 One asset of the adjustment layer is that if you make a mistake you can switch to white as the foreground color and repair the error. You can even save the image as a Photoshop file and return to the adjustment layer days later if you wish.

TIP

Vary the brush size and the opacity as you work, particularly where the sky meets the hills.

7 If you wanted to darken the sky still further, you could apply yet another adjustment layer, darken just the sky tones, and then mask the remainder of the picture. Flatten the image from the *Menu Bar* via *Layers* > **Flatten** to amalgamate the adjustment layer with the image to complete the manipulation.

ADJUSTING CONTRAST

Adjusting Exposure

UNDEREXPOSURE

OVEREXPOSURE

OPACITY SLIDER

BLEND MODES

BRIGHTNESS

If you are using a digital camera with an LCD screen, which gives you a preview of your images as you take them, under- and overexposure should be a rare occurrence. However, it does happen and you need to know how to deal with it as effectively as possible. Of course, the best option is to get the exposure right at the taking stage, but tricky lighting conditions can fool the light meters in our cameras from time to time.

There are several ways of dealing with exposure problems, but Photoshop Elements can guide you if you click the *How To* recipe tab from the *Palette Well*.

Fixing underexposure

Open an underexposed image and click the *How To* tab. From the drop-down menu, select *Fix > **Color and Brightness*** and then select *Fix the Exposure in a Photo*.

The recipe will tell you exactly how to proceed and will carry out some of the tasks for you if you wish. Click and drag your *Layers* palette from the *Palette Well* onto your desktop so you can observe what Elements is doing as you go through the process. As the *Layers* palette is now visible on screen, you can ignore step 1 in the recipe—it only opens the *Layers* palette for you.

2 A duplicate layer can be created manually from the *Menu Bar* via *Layer > **Duplicate Layer***, or by dragging the thumbnail of your image down the layers stack and dropping it over the center icon of the three on the bottom bar.

❷

3 From the drop-down blend modes, choose *Screen,* and you will notice a great improvement. You can fine-tune this process by reducing the *Opacity* in the *Layers* palette.

❶

❸

Following the recipe

You can make a duplicate layer of your underexposed image. using the manual method shown above. However, click Do This Step For Me in step 2 of the recipe and Elements will open up the Duplicate Layer box. You can type any name in this box and click OK. You will see that Elements has created your duplicate layer for you in your Layers palette.

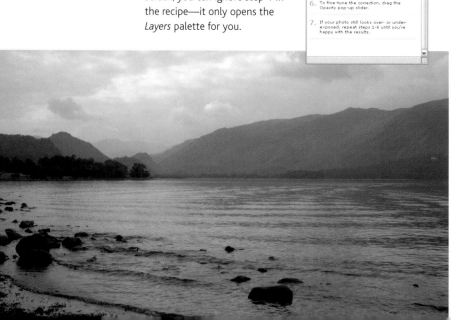

4 The results can be very good, but visit the *Quick Fix* tools for final adjustments and sharpening.

Finding new recipes

If you have an internet connection click the How To *tab and select* Download New Adobe Recipes. *You will be given the option to select just the recipes you want to add to those already located in Photoshop Elements. Your new recipes will show in the* New Items *section of the* How To *palette.*

②

Fixing overexposure

You can use the same recipe to correct overexposure, but remember that no process can bring back detail that is not in the original image.

2 Make your layer copy as you did with the underexposure example, but this time use *Multiply* from the drop-down blend modes and the *Opacity* slider to make any final adjustments.

①

Adjusting Colors

Photoshop Elements has provided us with a simple way to change the color in an image via the *Color Variations* palette, which is a little like the *Quick Fix* option. You can globally change the color or change selected areas if you make a selection first. See page 164 for some more details on how to go about this.

1 *Color Variations* is probably best applied to average key images where you are not looking to correct precise color, but where you want to affect the mood of an image. This example image fits into that category, where changes in precise color are not the object of the exercise.

2 The *Color Variations* command is found via *Enhance > Adjust Color > Color Variations*, but because this tool is likely to be used often, Elements has also included it as an icon on the *Shortcut* bar at the top of the screen.

    Color Variations is a very visual palette with a before-and-after thumbnail for you to monitor the effect of any changes you input. It is also rather like the *Quick Fix* options in that you can decide to accept the changes or not via the *OK* or *Undo* buttons before committing them to the image.

3 The amount of blue added is decided by the *Adjust Color Intensity* slider at the bottom left of the *Variations* palette. By default it is set midway along the slider bar.

4 With the example image on screen and without any changes to the default options in this palette you can click the button to *Increase Blue*. You will see that the *Color Variations* tool will add blue tone to the image and display the result in the *After* box.

5 Every time you click a thumbnail, Elements will add or subtract that color depending on what you have chosen. If the change is too great and you want a more subtle color, reduce the intensity with the *Color Intensity* slider before applying changes.

    The *Color Intensity* slider has six settings from a mild adjustment to a stronger intensity of color. In both these examples, the image has had just one click of red added, but from either end of the *Color Intensity* scale.

Tinting with Color Variations

This Color Variations *palette can also be used to add color to a monochrome image. In this monochrome example, I set the options to* Midtone *and with the intensity slider set midway, I increased the red by one click, decreased the blue by one click, and added one click of the* Darken *button.*

6 At any stage of your color experiments, you can reset your image back to its starting point by clicking the *Undo* button or by clicking the *Before* thumbnail.

If you reduce the *Color Intensity* slider to about one third value and hit the *Increase Blue* thumbnail again, you will see that the effect is far more subtle.

You can also affect other color changes by selecting *Midtones*, *Highlights,* or *Shadows* from the other option choices.

It is also possible to click more than one thumbnail to add multiples of color. With just a few clicks of those thumbnails, you can change the mood of your images quite significantly.

Emphasizing Color

Many of your images can be improved in a variety of ways, and that is the main concern of this book. One of those ways is to enhance the color, but do so only when the image demands it. If you overdo your increases in color saturation or use it on the wrong subject, your images can look unappealing and false.

Color manipulation can be fun, and here we'll explore two ways of emphasizing color that can create a dynamic image. The *Hue and Saturation* palette can be used for most images if they require only subtle changes in color, while there is a technique using the *Color* blend mode that works well where a more forceful effect is required.

Increasing saturation

1 This image is crying out for an injection of color to bring out the impact of the rusty legs of the pier.

2 The simplest way to achieve this is by selecting *Enhance > Adjust Color > **Hue and Saturation*** from the *Menu Bar* at the top of the screen.

3 Move the *Saturation* slider gently to the right to squeeze as much color into the subject as you can.

Using the Color blend mode

1 If we really want to push the color saturation high for a particular reason, we can use another technique as we have with this close-up shot of a traction engine.

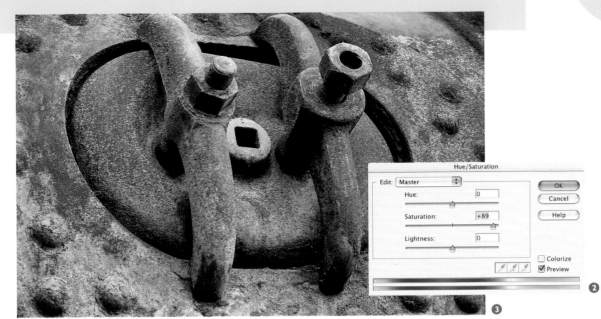

2 You need a duplicate layer for this technique. Select *Layer > **Duplicate Layer*** from the *Menu Bar* and click *OK* from the *Duplicate Layer* box. Select the *Hue and Saturation* palette again and this time use the shortcut Ctrl+U to bring up the palette. Move the *Saturation* slider most of the way to the right to inject some serious color into the subject.

3 This process also introduces some unwanted side effects, such as a heavy pixel effect. This is unattractive, but can be fixed.

4 From the *Menu Bar* select *Filters > Noise > **Median*** and add about a 10 pixel *Radius*, just enough to smooth out those unattractive speckles. Click the *Layers* tab from the *Palette Well* and from the drop-down blend modes select *Color*. Elements will blend the color layer with the original and you get the best of both worlds.

5 Reducing the *Opacity* slider in the *Layers* palette will reduce the color if it is too high, but the object of this exercise was to deliberately overemphasize the color.

To continue any further manipulations with an image like this, such as darkening the outer edges, select *Layer > **Flatten*** from the *Menu Bar* to flatten both layers together.

AUTO COLOR

COLOR VARIATIONS

FREEHAND LASSO

DESATURATION

COLOR BALANCE

Removing a Color Cast

Cameras, whether they are digital or film, are calibrated for color so that they give the best color results at noon daylight. If you shoot late in the day or early morning, the color balance is much warmer and it is this effect that produces those lovely warm sunset colors.

While this color change works in our favor sometimes, it can do the exact opposite when shooting under fluorescent or tungsten light with your digital camera set for cloudy or bright conditions.

In this example, the image had to be grabbed while the animal was close enough for a dramatic shot, but it was shot under fluorescent light and the result has an all-over green cast. You can remove such casts or at least greatly improve them using Photoshop Elements. You are unlikely to be able to make a one-click global change, but rather a series of small changes.

2 Click the *Quick Fix* icon from the *Shortcut Bar* and from the palette click *Color Correction > Auto Color > Apply* and you will see a considerable change in the color. Click *OK* to accept the change or experiment with other *Quick Fix* options.

3 Click the *Color Variations* icon from the *Shortcut Bar* and from the options select *Saturation*. You can click the *More Saturation* option to add some instant color back into the iguana.

4 The iguana's eye needs some attention too; it needs to be lightened a little. You can do that by selecting the *Freehand Lasso* tool from the *Toolbar* and making a selection of just the eye. From the *Menu Bar*, choose *Select > Feather* and add about 3 pixels of feather to the selection line. This will ensure that your changes are unseen.

5 Select the *Levels* command from the *Menu Bar* via *Enhance > Adjust Brightness > Contrast > Levels* and move the right-hand slider that represents the light pixels toward the left to lighten the eye. You will need to remove the selection on the eye via the shortcut Ctrl+D.

The result is now far better, but the background is holding the impact of the image back.

6 Make a selection around the outside edge of the iguana and feather the selection by 2–3 pixels. Using the *Clone* tool and with the image greatly enlarged, you can carefully clone around the background to tidy up those light distracting areas.

You need to remove some of the color from the background, which you can do with the *Sponge* tool. Select the *Sponge* tool from the *Toolbar* and from the *Options Bar* select a mode of *Desaturate* and a *Flow* of around 50%.

7 Gradually remove the green color from the background so that the color does not overpower the image. How far you take this is a personal choice, but the result can only be an improvement.

Removing Red Eye

Red eye can turn even the sweetest child into a demon, long before their teenage years. The problem occurs when light from an on-camera flash reflects off the blood vessels at the back of the subject's eyes. Despite the best efforts of camera manufacturers to eliminate it, it remains a common fault in portrait shots.

I In fact, red eye is so common that Elements has a tool specifically designed to deal with it: the *Red Eye* brush. It's one of the easiest and most effective tools in the program. There are a number of options that come up on the *Options Bar* when the tool is selected, but don't be daunted by them. If you work through this process step by step you will see how simple it is to use.

2 Using the *Zoom* tool from the *Toolbar*, enlarge the eyes in the image so that they fill the screen. The *Red Eye* brush is far easier to apply with the image greatly enlarged and you will also be able to evaluate your work better.

Select the *Red Eye* brush from the *Toolbar* and a soft-edged brush from the *Options Bar*. The pixel radius of the brush needs to be just a little larger than the size of the red pupil. If you look at the *Options Bar* you will see that the sampling box says *First Click*. This means that the first click down on the picture surface will select the color you want to eradicate—in this instance, the red pupils of the eye.

Touch down on the center of a pupil and the red color will be sampled and selected.

3 You can then paint out the red eye using the default settings. This usually entails only a single click of the mouse. With this example, I changed the minimum of options but the results were excellent.

However, you can select a replacement color for the eye, or use the tool to enhance the original eye color of the person in the photo.

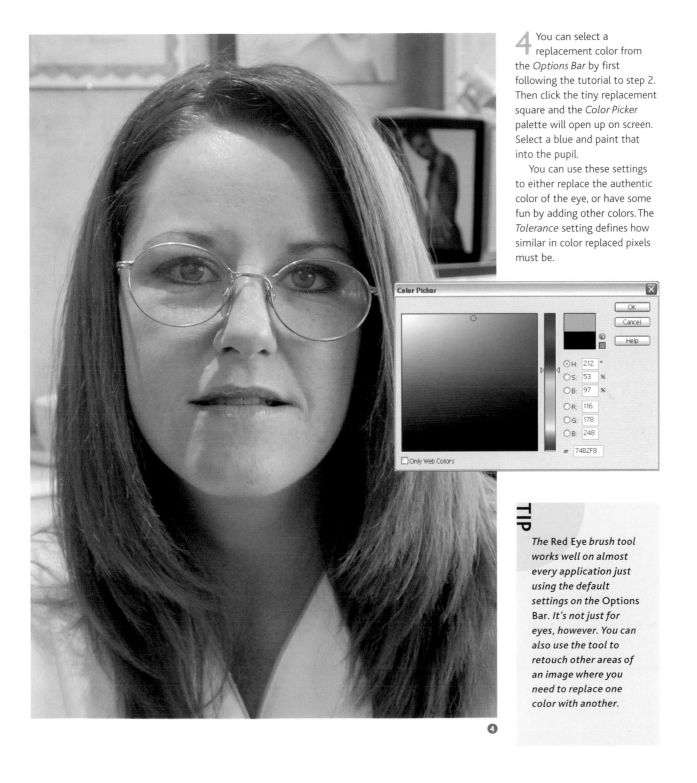

4 You can select a replacement color from the *Options Bar* by first following the tutorial to step 2. Then click the tiny replacement square and the *Color Picker* palette will open up on screen. Select a blue and paint that into the pupil.

You can use these settings to either replace the authentic color of the eye, or have some fun by adding other colors. The *Tolerance* setting defines how similar in color replaced pixels must be.

TIP

The Red Eye *brush tool works well on almost every application just using the default settings on the* Options Bar. *It's not just for eyes, however. You can also use the tool to retouch other areas of an image where you need to replace one color with another.*

Sharpening

One of the most misunderstood tools in Photoshop Elements is the *Unsharp Mask* (USM) from the *Filters* menu. The name of the tool alone can be misleading—it doesn't "unsharpen" anything, but is named after a traditional photographic technique used to sharpen edges.

This is one of those tools where a little technical information will help you to understand it better. The sharpening tools work by increasing the levels of contrast between adjacent pixels. Although there are other sharpness tools in the *Filter* menu, the *Unsharp Mask* tool affords the most control.

❶

| This example was taken in the pouring rain using a 6 megapixel digital camera. The first task is to enlarge the image using the *Zoom* tool. This allows you to see the effect of the sharpening as you apply the tool.

This enlargement can be an important point because the *Unsharp Mask* tool can be overdone. The consequence is a visible deterioration of the image quality. You need to squeeze as much *Unsharp Mask* into your images as you can without introducing the negative effects of the tool.

2 From the *Menu Bar* select *Filters > Sharpen > Unsharp Mask.* Elements will bring up the *Unsharp Mask* palette, with a preview window and three control sliders.

3 Drag the *Amount* slider to about 150–200% to determine by how much to increase the contrast. This amount is generally the recommended standard setting.

Drag the *Radius* slider to the right or type in a value in the box provided. For high-resolution images of around 5–6 million pixels use a setting of 1–2. For lower-resolution shots (around 3 million pixels) a lower radius may be necessary.

The *Threshold* slider determines how different pixels must be from the surrounding area before they are considered edge pixels. In practice, low values produce a good result.

TIP

Once you have applied your settings, click the preview box in the USM *palette on and off while looking at the main image on screen to see the before-and-after effect. This will help you to appreciate not only the positive aspects of the* USM *tool, but also the negative ones that creep in if you increase the radius too far.*

❷

❸

Although it is vital to use the USM tool carefully, in the right circumstances it can totally transform some images.

With animal subjects, the fur can often stand far more sharpening than the smoother tones of a background. In those circumstances, you can make a selection of what you wish to sharpen and add a few pixels of Feather. Apply the sharpening tool only to the main subject.

TIP

Each image will react slightly differently to the Unsharp Mask, *but once you get a good average setting for the resolution of your camera, the basic settings will remain in the palette each time it is called up. After that you just need to make small changes to suit the subject.*

This works particularly well on images that have a blurred background: the sort of background you may get when photographing an animal from a distance using the zoom lens. In these cases, you can get the maximum sharpening of the fur without affecting the smooth tones of the background.

photo retouching
techniques

By now you should be familiar with the basic tools that Photoshop Elements offers to fix common photographic faults. But Elements has more up its sleeve than that. With the aid of some more advanced features, you can interactively retouch your photos, removing ugly marks or scratches, introducing new effects, or tweaking areas of color and tone to add impact to the composition. This chapter also reveals how you can use Elements to bring old photos back to life.

Removing Small Blemishes

blemishes

GARDENING

CLONE STAMP TOOL

BRUSH SIZE

SOFT-EDGED BRUSH

SAMPLING

From time to time you will need to remove small marks and blemishes that appear on your pictures. With some digital SLR cameras that have removable lenses you can get the odd speck of dust inside the camera, which may result in a small, out-of-focus shadow on the picture.

However, more often than not the small blemishes you need to remove are not camera faults at all, but man-made objects in the landscape that reduce the appeal of the picture. Discarded litter, TV antennas, and other unwanted clutter can spoil your images. Sometimes it is not possible to appreciate how badly these affect your shot until you get rid of these ugly distractions and compare the images before·and after.

This type of work is often referred to as "gardening" in photographic circles. To do your "gardening," you need an appropriate tool, and the main tool for this type of work is the Clone Stamp *from the* Toolbar. *The* Clone *tool, as it's usually called, is probably one of the most well-used within any version of Photoshop or Photoshop Elements. If you look at the* Options Bar *along the top of the screen, you will see that this tool has many options. The only option you need to concern yourself with at this stage is the brush size.*

❶

| This image looks pretty good, but look again at all the clutter in the water. To save money, local fisherman have used plastic bottles as floats to tie up their boats and these rather spoil the charm of the picture. While the white bottles may be less evident at small print sizes or on screen, they would certainly be evident at double Letter size.

❷

2 Select the *Zoom* tool from the *Toolbar* and enlarge the image to about 200%. At this level of enlargement you can deal with each of these distractions more effectively.

Select the *Clone Stamp* tool and choose your brush size. This will depend on the size of the blemish you wish to deal with. Try to select a brush size that is similar in size to the blemish if possible. Make sure you select a soft-edged brush so your cloned pixels blend into the picture well. You need to ensure that your work is undetectable.

TIP

Use the [and] keys to the right of the P key on your keyboard to scroll up and down the brush sizes. This saves you continually having to go to the Options Bar *to change brush size.*

❸

3 You can use the *Clone* tool to remove the blemishes and also remove the cranes up on the skyline to the right. How much *"gardening"* you do is a personal choice, but remember that attention to detail is what makes images stand out from the rest. In this example, I decided to remove a boat or two as well.

4 Hold down the Alt key and the clone cursor will change to a sample cursor. If you left-click over a part of the image, an area of color and texture the same size as your brush will be sampled. Thought needs to be given to where you sample from, so that you paint in the right tone and texture.

In this example, the correct place is just to the left or right of the white plastic bottles in line with the waves on the water. Left-click to make the sample and then release the Alt key and move over the edge of a plastic bottle. Left-click again and the pixels you sampled will be painted over the plastic bottle, concealing it.

Try to use separate clicks rather than a painting stroke. If you use a painting stroke, you may introduce an odd effect that looks like snakeskin. This is caused when you sample an

already sampled area. The sampled pixels are repeated in a pattern that soon becomes easily visible. Release the left mouse and change the sample point often and this effect will be minimized, making your work practically undetectable.

TIP

With the picture enlarged, hold down the space bar and the cursor will change to the **Hand** *tool. Left-click and drag while holding the space bar and you can move your enlarged image along to the next blemish. This is a great way to navigate around an enlarged picture.*

This technique can be used on a wide variety of images and subjects. In this image of a castle, the distractions are either man-made objects or people, but they can all be removed using the Clone *tool.*

Removing Scratches and Dirt

One of the great advantages of digital photography is the fact that images from a digital camera are usually so clean. You get none of the problems that you can experience with film, such as scratches on the negative, dust scanned in with the print, or watermarks from the original processing. Once you start scanning in your best pre-digital efforts, however, all these problems soon come flooding back. If you want to retain and restore the best of your old photographs, you still need to find a way to remove these ugly blemishes.

When there are only a few marks on a picture, you can usually deal with them using the *Clone* tool, but sometimes a photo is too dirty to make that process worthwhile. As tempting as it is to give up and throw a problem image away, an irreplaceable family photo is not easily discarded. Instead, you can salvage that treasured photo with another Elements tool: the *Dust and Scratches* filter.

▼ *Any collection of scanned 35mm prints, slides, or negatives will throw up a few examples where dust, dirt, processing, or careless handling have taken their toll. This example is in awful condition, which makes it perfect for our tutorial.*

Cleaning up the marks and scratches is a simple process, but there are downsides to it. Any filter that removes several scratches in a single pass will do so at the cost of sharpness. Whether the remedy assists the situation or makes matters worse depends on the image and its problems, but as the cleaning process is such a quick one, little is lost by trying and evaluating the result. It is not until you look at an image enlarged at 100% that you can see what you are up against.

Go to the *Menu Bar* and select *Filter > Noise > **Dust and Scratches*** and Elements will present you with the options dialog for the filter. Keep the image enlarged in the preview window, so that you can see the effect of the filter as you adjust the options. Click and drag the thumbnail in the preview window if you need to see another part of the image.

In this example, the marks are so widespread that you should apply the filter to the whole image. If only a portion is affected, select that area using the *Marquee* or *Lasso* tools before applying the filter.

Start the process by sliding the *Threshold* slider left to 0. The *Threshold* setting determines how sensitive the filter is to the marks on the image. Move it above 0 to limit the filter's effects if it is over-softening the image.

Dust & Scratches

OK
Cancel
☑ Preview

100%

Radius: 5 pixels

Threshold: 0 levels

❷

2 Drag the *Radius* slider to the right or type a value into the box and observe the effect of the adjustment.

In this example, a 3 pixel *Radius* helps the situation, but does not entirely deal with all the dirt on the slide. For this shot, you would need to move the *Radius* up to 5 to get an acceptable result.

The final result looks a lot cleaner, but you can see that the filter process has taken some of the sharpness from the image. You can decrease the softening effect by moving the *Threshold* slider to the right. In this case, however, it doesn't assist very much before the scratches start to reappear.

Dust & Scratches

OK
Cancel
☑ Preview

100%

Radius: 3 pixels

levels

Unsharp Mask

OK
Cancel
☑ Preview

100%

Amount: 200 %

Radius: 3 pixels

Threshold: 0 levels

❸

TIP

A good way to evaluate many of the tools in Photoshop Elements is to enter your first choices into the options and click the Preview · *checkbox on and off. Jumping between the examples before and after makes it far easier to adjust the settings and get the best results for the image.*

3 If the *Threshold* slider can't help, there is another solution. Go to the *Menu Bar* and select *Filter > Sharpen > **Unsharp Mask***. Keep the *Amount* at 200% and the *Threshold* at 0, but use a 3 pixel *Radius*. This brings back some of the sharpness without undoing the effect of the *Dust and Scratches* filter.

Using this technique has softened the image, but you can easily live with the results. If the image is an important family picture, it's well worth making such a small sacrifice.

Dodging and Burning

The term "burning" comes from a darkroom technique in which more exposure is given to one part of the printing paper to make it darker than the rest.

In the reverse of this technique, "dodging," light is held back from falling on a part of the photographic paper in order to lighten it.

To use these tools effectively there are some options that you need to know about, most importantly the *Range* and *Exposure* settings. Use the first to select which tones the tool works on, and the second to increase or decrease the level of the tool's effect.

2 If you click the *Range* drop-down menu, you will see that you can use these tools on either the highlights, shadows, or midtones within a picture. It is a great benefit to be able to adjust these tones one at a time.

These tools are best used with the *Exposure* set fairly low —around 5% or even lower. Any higher and the effect can be too harsh and obvious. To be effective, changes made with these tools need to be subtle and seamless.

1 To darken an area in an image, as in this example, you first need to enlarge the image using the *Zoom* tool. Then select the *Burn* tool from the *Toolbar* and set the *Range* option to *Highlights* and the *Exposure* to 5%.

You can gradually *Burn* (darken) the tones in the white feathers around the bottom of the picture. If you are using this tool for the first time, you may feel that work is progressing too slowly and be tempted to increase the exposure. You can get away with that sometimes, but a subtle approach usually gets better results.

3 Switch the *Burn* tool to *Shadows* or *Midtones* and you can affect those tones in exactly the same way. You can use the *Burn* tool at the top of the image as well. The process hasn't got rid of the out-of-focus letters in the background completely, but it has reduced their prominence.

TIP

Don't try to use the Burn *tool set for* Highlights *on areas of a picture where there is no detail at all. The effect is usually just an ugly gray splotch. This tool needs some detail and tone to work with. If you have a problem area with no tone at all, you need to use a different option. Try using the* Clone *tool to copy in some detail.*

The Dodge *tool works in exactly the same way, but lightens tones. With this image, you will see that even after altering the* Levels, *some areas of the picture could do with lightening. The* Dodge *tool is perfect for this task.*

Select the Dodge *tool from the* Toolbar *and use the same settings as described for the* Burn *tool. Choose a low* Exposure *setting and select* Highlights *as your* Range *choice.*

Use these settings carefully to avoid overdoing the dodging effect. This causes the highlights to burn out by removing the detail completely. The effects of the Dodge *tool are often more subtle than the* Burn *tool; it has been used here to highlight the sparkle on the water.*

DODGING AND BURNING

Soft-focus Effects

Soft-focus has always been a popular addition to portraits, particularly female portraits. In conventional photography the technique required special filters. In Photoshop Elements, however, we can do without the special equipment and emulate the soft-focus style using a combination of layers and filter effects.

> *Soft-focus effects used to be created using optical filters, either fitted to the lens when taking the photo or employed in the darkroom afterward. Photoshop Elements can emulate this soft effect. Like the old method, it is typically applied to female portraits.*

1 Layers are crucial to the creation of the soft-focus look, so begin by clicking the *Layers* tab from the *Palette Well* to open the *Layers* palette. You need to make a duplicate of the background layer by selecting *Layer > **Duplicate Layer***.

Alternatively, click and drag the thumbnail down and drop it on the central copy icon at the base of the *Layers* palette. Elements will create the layer copy for you.

2 Select *Blur > **Gaussian Blur*** from the *Filters* menu and select a *Radius* of about 10 pixels. This setting will vary depending on the size and content of the image, so experiment with higher and lower *Radius* settings until you get an effective soft-focus look on the skin and the hair. The effect after running the *Blur* filter is not completely flattering, as the filter blurs everything. The next simple step will fix that.

3 Go to the *Layers* palette and click on the *Opacity* slider, then reduce the *Opacity* to about 50%. Different settings suit different images, so reduce or increase the *Opacity* to arrive at an effect that pleases you.

The result of these manipulations is now very pleasant, with a delicate softness that you can tweak further using the *Opacity* slider.

4 The one downside to this technique is that it takes away the sharpness of the eyes. However, you can fix that too if you wish. Enlarge the eyes using the *Zoom* tool from the *Toolbar*, then select the standard *Eraser* tool. Go up to the *Options Bar* and choose an *Opacity* setting of around 10% and a brush size about a quarter the size of the eye.

Make sure that the upper layer in the *Layers* palette is selected and ready for editing, then erase the eyes from the *Gaussian Blur* layer, working gently to reveal the crisp detail in the layer below.

TIP

Hit the M key on your keyboard and then the number 5 key and Elements will reduce the Opacity *of the layer to 50%. Use the 6 key instead and the* Opacity *becomes 60%; 7 equals 70%; and so on up to for 100% (the 0 key).*

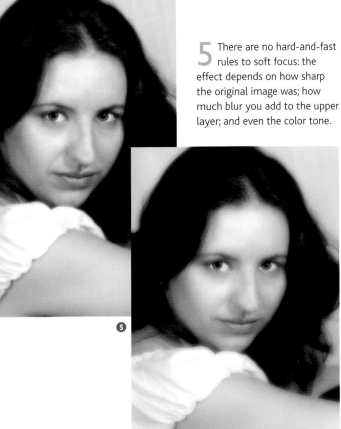

5 There are no hard-and-fast rules to soft focus: the effect depends on how sharp the original image was; how much blur you add to the upper layer; and even the color tone.

Soft focus can also be used on animals, but with slightly less Gaussian Blur *and a lower* Opacity *for the blur layer. This gives a delicate and attractive quality to fur and feathers. As with the portraits, you can also use the* Eraser *to ensure that important parts remain sharp.*

Sharpening and Blurring a Selected Area

There are several ways in which you can affect just one part of an image using the tools of Photoshop Elements. The vast majority of the time you would make a selection of the area you wanted to edit. However, there is an alternative in the shape of the *Blur* and *Sharpen* tools, which are located on the *Toolbar*.

The difference with these tools from those found in the *Filter* menu is that you can apply the effect via a brush and control the strength of the brush from the *Options Bar*. You can apply just the amount of sharpness or blur you require in the precise location you need it.

The *Blur* tool can be useful in portrait images where you may wish to soften some isolated folds or lines in the skin.

In this example, the statue does not stand out from the background that well. You can rectify this with the Blur and Sharpen tools, using them both on the same image.

As with most of the Brush tools, you should make your changes with the image greatly enlarged. The first step, therefore, is to enlarge the image to around 200% using the Zoom tool.

Select the Blur tool from the Toolbar along with a soft-edged brush. The strength setting will vary depending on what you wish to blur and by how much; for this example, I set it quite high. The brush size needs to be small enough not to encroach on the parts you do not want to blur. You can then carefully blur just one area of the image —in this case, the cut-out shape in the wall behind the statue.

Now select the Sharpen tool from the Toolbar and apply it to the statue. This will make the statue stand out even more from the blurred background. Once again, you need the image to be greatly enlarged to enable you to work more easily.

TIP

With the image greatly enlarged, you can move around it by holding down the space bar so the Hand tool appears. You can then click and drag the image along to the next area you wish to manipulate. Release the space bar and the Blur tool will return.

TIP

The strength setting for the Sharpen tool is a little more critical than the Blur tool, so start off with a low-strength setting. It is much easier to overdo the Sharpening tool than the Blur tool, and the "blocky" result is quite obvious.

Quite often in digital photography you will need to combine tools for a better end result. This was the case with this insect picture. I used the Blur tool to blur the leaves closest to the insect, switching to the Sharpen tool to sharpen just the insect. What also enhanced this image was a selective darkening of the leaves using the Burn tool.

Depth of Field Effects

When you take photographs with a telephoto lens or move in toward your subject for some close-up photography, you expect the background of the subject to be blurred. We call this effect depth of field. While it has its downside, it can be used to add a sense of depth to an image or separate a subject from the background.

Mimicking depth of field

I You can recreate this effect digitally by emphasizing one part of an image. In this shot of the interior of a hot air balloon, you can recreate depth of field by adding *Gaussian Blur* to certain areas.

2 From the *Menu Bar*, select *Layer* > **Duplicate Layer** and then click *OK* in the *Duplicate Layer* dialog that appears on the screen.

Go to the *Menu Bar* again and select *Filter* > *Blur* > *Gaussian Blur* and then add a pixel *Radius* of between 5 and 10 pixels.

3 If you click on the *Layers* tab from the *Palette Well*, you can see that the original sharp layer is at the bottom of the layers stack and the blurred one above.

Now select the *Eraser* tool from the *Toolbar* and erase the bottom third of that blurred layer and the man who forms the center of interest. This will leave the sharp layer beneath showing through in all the right places. Select *Layers* > **Flatten** when complete.

Easy depth of field

1 From the *Menu Bar* go to *Select > **Feather*** and add a 150 pixel *Radius* to the selection line. From the filters, you can apply the *Gaussian Blur* filter again to complete the effect.

2 In this second example, you can apply *Gaussian Blur* much more easily by selecting the *Rectangular Marquee* tool from the *Toolbar* and making a selection of the right-hand side of the image.

Isolate the subject

Depth of field is determined mainly by the lens, choice of aperture and the distance from the subject. In most cases, it works in your favor as it isolates the main center of interest against an out-of-focus background. It also makes images more dynamic in the picture space. The example here demonstrates this effect well.

Saturating and Desaturating Color in a Selected Area

Some of your images may need to be improved by introducing extra color into a particular area of the picture or by removing some depth of color from another part. You can use the *Selection* tools for this type of work, or you can use another tool in the Photoshop Elements armory and avoid selections completely.

An alternative tool is the *Sponge* tool, which is found on the *Toolbar*. Select the *Sponge* tool and look up to the top of the screen at the *Options Bar*. You will see that there are relatively few options with this tool. Under the *Mode* setting, there are two options: *Saturate* and *Desaturate*. The *Desaturate* option removes color and the *Saturate* option increases color. Rather than affect the whole image or make a selection, you can use a brush to affect just a small area of the picture.

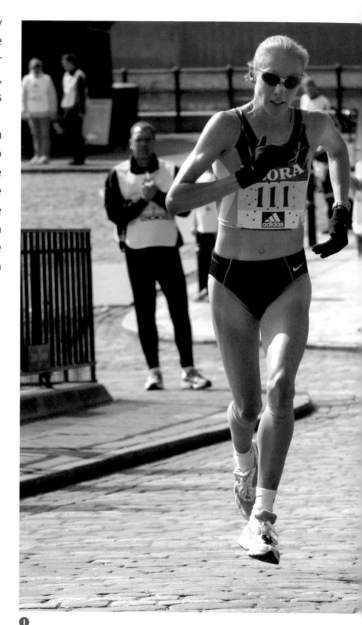

This shot shows the women's winner of the 2002 London Marathon. While taking photographs of the event, I got really annoyed with the marshals along the course; there seemed to be thousands of them, all wearing lime-green jackets. They were continually getting in the way of a clear view of the runners.

There are eight marshals in this picture and they spoiled almost every shot that I took. However, this picture can be used to demonstrate how the *Sponge* tool can improve an image. I used it set to the *Desaturate* mode to remove the brightness of the color from the marshals' jackets.

2 Starting with the two figures top left, use the *Zoom* tool to enlarge the image so that the subjects are large enough to work on.

From the options, choose a mode of *Desaturate* and select a soft-edged brush with a diameter of about 40–60 pixels.

Adjust the *Flow* of the tool from the *Options Bar* and vary the brush size depending on what part of the image you are working on. For this particular task the *Flow* can be kept quite high given the bright color of the jackets, so you can start comfortably at 50%.

Gradually desaturate these two green jackets so that they are less intrusive in the picture, then do the same with the rest of the green jackets.

Increasing the saturation involves the same techniques that you have already used for the desaturating option. With this example, you could in fact employ both tools—one to desaturate the outer parts and the other to saturate the inner parts of the gold plaque.

From the Options Bar, *select the* Saturation *option to add color to the raised figure on the plaque. You need to work with the image greatly enlarged and adjust your brush size so that you can work comfortably. This tool is quick and easy to use without the need for complicated selections.*

3 You could also use the *Burn* tool after desaturating the color of the jackets to darken them down still further.

Fixing Converging Verticals

Pictures from vacation destinations must account for millions of frames a year, be they digital or film. When we go to major places of interest it can sometimes be difficult to find a new angle on popular subjects. With so many great images from around the world filling our newspapers and magazines we can be forgiven for giving up before we start. We don't always have the advantage of that privileged viewpoint or a range of lenses to die for, but all is not lost.

Try looking for something a little different from the norm and you may be surprised with the results. I shot this picture of Sydney Harbour Bridge across the bay toward Sydney Opera House, but chose to shoot through the Harbour Bridge. I had to shoot upward with a wide-angle lens to avoid distracting parked cars, but that then caused the verticals to badly distort in the picture.

The tools of Photoshop Elements come to the rescue. You can make use of the *Transform* tools to straighten up the converging verticals.

2 With the image on screen, open the *Layers* palette from the *Palette Well* and change the default background into a layer. You can do this by simply double-clicking the thumbnail and renaming the layer in the *New Layer* box.

3 From the *Menu Bar*, select *Image > Transform > Distort* and Elements will place a bounding box around the whole image.

Drag the toggle at the top left corner out toward the left and the right toggle out toward the right until you see that the verticals are straight.

4 If you click and drag the center toggle at the bottom of the bounding box downward a little, you can get rid of those distracting cars at the same time.

⑤

5 Click the tick on the *Options Bar* or hit *Enter* and Elements will correct the verticals for you.

At the end of the process, you will need to go to the *Menu Bar* and select *Layer > **Flatten*** to return the layer to the background.

TIP

With the Distort Transform tool selected, you can either drag out the toggles left and right separately or hold down the Alt key, the Ctrl key, and the Shift key together and the bounding box can be dragged out identically on both sides.

TIP

You will need room around the image to drag out those toggles and straighten the verticals. If your image fills the monitor, you may need to make the image smaller. There is no need to change to the Zoom tool for this task. Hold down the Alt key and the space bar together and the Minus Zoom tool appears. Click into the image to reduce the size. Release those keys and the bounding box will still be in place ready for your manipulations.

By using the same techniques on this image, it is possible to drag the bounding box upward to give the castle more height and power as well as fixing the verticals.

*If you want the verticals to be absolutely straight, select View > **Grid** from the Menu Bar and use the upright lines as a guide for the Transform tools.*

Deliberate Distortion Tricks

Some of the most simple subjects can provide great images, and what more everyday object can you find than a fork? Where do you start to be creative with an image like this? Use the *Distortion* tools that are found in the *Filters* menu and you can add a new twist—literally—to what might seem like a mundane subject.

The first task with a project is to remove the black background from the fork in order to create a transparency —i.e. to have the fork floating on a transparent background. The similarity of tones in this image makes it difficult to use the automatic selection tools like the *Magic Wand*. Instead, use the *Polygonal Lasso* tool from the *Toolbar*. Working with the image enlarged to about 200–300% makes the selection task easier, so make use of the *Zoom* tool first.

2 To make a selection around the fork, left-click with the *Polygonal Lasso* tool on the edge of the fork and work around the fork in stages, clicking down in short steps. The steps can be longer on the straight edges, but use lots of short lines for the curves. With the image well enlarged this is a fairly easy task.

3 From the *Menu Bar*, choose *Select > **Feather*** and add a 1 pixel *Feather* to the *Selection*. Then go to *Select > **Inverse*** to inverse the selection; Elements now selects the black background rather than the fork. Change the background into a layer by double-clicking the thumbnail from the layers palette and renaming it. Then choose *Edit > **Cut*** and you have your transparency.

4 Once you have the fork transparency we can start some real improvements. The fork is dull, so you need to go to the *Levels* palette or the *Quick Fix* option to apply *Levels*. Then, from the *Menu Bar*, select *Enhance > Adjust Color > **Hue and Saturation*** and add some serious color to the fork.

5 At this stage you need to increase the canvas size; you can do that from the *Menu Bar*. Select *Image > Resize > **Canvas Size*** and *Anchor* the image to the left. Increase the canvas *Width* by a few inches.

6 From the *Menu Bar* you now need to create a new blank layer via *Layer > **New Layer***. You can select a name for the layer or just click *OK*. From within the *Layers* palette, left-click and drag that new blank layer beneath the fork and flood it with black using the *Paint Bucket* tool from the *Toolbar*. This will give you a better idea of how the image is coming together than looking at the tiny blue and white squares will.

Deliberate Distortion Tricks continued

distortion

8 From the *Menu Bar* select *Filters > Distort > **Wave*** and adjust the sliders to give a nice curved and distorted look to the prong.

7 If you select the fork layer and select the *Freehand Lasso* tool, you can make a selection of the far right prong of the fork. Feather the edge of the selection by about 10 pixels and then choose *Edit > **Cut*** and *Edit > **Paste*** from the *Menu Bar*. Elements will *Paste* the prong to a new layer.

9 Select *Free Transform* from the *Menu Bar* and you can then position the prong back into place and adjust the size to hide the join.

10 Another element is needed to complete the image; what better than the bold color of a tomato? Open the image and prepare it as a transparency in the same way that you did with the original fork. The *Magic Wand* will be able to cope, given the contrast between the tomato and the background.

11 Once you have the tomato prepared, select the *Move* tool from the *Toolbar*, click into the tomato image, and drag and drop it into the fork image to make another layer. Now you can position the tomato anywhere in the frame you wish. With a little work with the *Eraser* tool, you can create the effect of the tomato being pierced by the fork.

12 Look at the *Layers* palette, and you will see the layers and how this image has been built up. You can create a more dramatic background using the *Gradient* tool to complete the dynamic image.

Removing Unwanted Objects

CUT AND PASTE

FREEHAND LASSO

FEATHER RADIUS

ERASER TOOL

CLONE TOOL

In the course of your photography you will find that you cannot frame a shot as you would like. For example, in this picture of the harbor area in Hong Kong, the skyscrapers and the cruise ship have considerable impact, but the overall image is spoiled by the ropes tying up the ship to the dockside.

The tools of Photoshop Elements can be used to completely remove disfiguring distractions such as the ropes. There are two techniques you can employ for this type of problem, and you will often find that you need to use them in combination.

Patching and cloning

In our example we should first look at the docking ropes at the point where they cross the bow of the ship into the sea. While it might be tempting to reach straight for the *Clone* tool, it would be difficult to use in this situation. If you turn to a cut-and-paste technique you can do a better, more controlled job.

2 Enlarge the image to something like 300–400%, concentrating on the part of the bow where the ropes cross.

3 Using the *Freehand Lasso* tool from the *Toolbar*, make a selection of both the bow of the ship and the water, being sure to select above where the rope crosses.

From the *Menu Bar*, go to *Select > **Feather*** and add a 10 pixel *Feather Radius*. This ensures that the selection, when copied, is soft and easy to merge with the remainder of the ship. From the *Menu Bar*, choose *Edit > **Copy*** and then *Edit > **Paste*** and Elements will paste the selected pixels to a new layer.

4 What you have done with this procedure is to create a patch on a new layer. Click the *Layers* tab from the *Palette Well* and you will see the patch layer you have created.

5 Select the *Move* tool from the *Toolbar* and move the newly created patch down over the rope, lining up the patch with the edge of the ship.

If the feathered edge that you created for the bow edge of the ship needs any help to merge into the ship, use the *Eraser* tool on the patch layer. Make sure that the *Opacity* is set very low, to around 5%. You also need a soft-edged brush.

Save the image as a standard Photoshop layered file with the extension .PSD. You can then flatten these two layers together by selecting *Layers > **Flatten***.

6

6 You need the *Clone* tool next from the *Toolbar*, but for this task you are going to clone to a new blank layer. To achieve this, you need to create it from the *Menu Bar* via *Layer > **New Blank Layer***.

From the *Option* bar of the *Clone* tool, tick the *Use All Layers* box. This allow you to sample textures and colors from the ship layer and paint those pixels onto the new blank layer. The benefit of cloning to a new blank layer is that you never apply changes to the original ship layer. All your cloning appears on the blank layer, which in turn allows you to ensure that your work is seamless before you combine the layers together. This is a great way to work as any mistakes can easily be erased.

Using the *Clone* tool, sample close to the area we want to clone, by holding down the Alt key and left-clicking the mouse. Release the Alt key and apply the sampled pixels over the other parts of the rope.

TIP

Change the sample point often and try to avoid making one sample and using that for the entire job. This method does work sometimes, but a more random approach produces more natural-looking results.

7 Start with the bow of the ship and then move onto the sea area. Because of the texture and colors of the sea, the cloning should be easy to conceal. Continue along the remainder of the rope.

7

A similar technique was used on this more old-fashioned nautical shot. In this example, the Clone tool made swift work of the ropes, but it also came in useful for deleting the intrusive quay. The rougher texture of the water was harder to match with a simple patch. With a contrast adjustment via Levels, the final result is far more pleasing to the eye.

FEATHER RADIUS

DUPLICATE LAYER

MAGIC WAND

TOLERANCE

FREE TRANSFORM

Copying Objects

Another way of improving images is by copying objects from one image to another, or within the same image. This is particularly useful when an otherwise attractive shot lacks a strong focal point to draw the eye. You could also take just one object and copy that to form an entire picture, as we've done in the example image below.

1 To start the process, you need to change the background into a layer from the *Layers* palette by double-clicking the thumbnail and renaming it.

2 You first need to remove the sky from the aircraft image using the *Magic Wand* tool from the *Toolbar*. From the *Options Bar*, select a *Tolerance* of 32 and click into the sky. Most of the sky will be selected; any that is not can be added to by holding the Shift key and clicking in the unselected areas.

3 From the *Menu Bar* choose *Select > Feather* and add a 1 pixel *Feather* to the selection. From the *Edit* menu select *Cut*. (You can also use the shortcut Ctrl+X for this cut command.) You will see from the checkerboard effect that the sky area is now transparent.

Now turn the single aircraft into a squadron of aircraft by copying it. Click the *Layers* tab from the *Palette Well*, open the *Layers* palette, and drag the thumbnail down the *Layers* palette and drop it over the center copy icon at the bottom. Elements will make a duplicate for you, which you can see shown as a thumbnail in the *Layers* palette.

4 You will not be able to see the other aircraft on screen until you select the *Move* tool from the *Toolbar* and move one of them aside. The copy process places the copied aircraft directly over the top of the original in perfect register.

5 To change the size of the planes, go to the *Menu Bar* and select *Image > Transform > Free Transform* or use the shortcut Ctrl+T. Elements places a bounding box around the aircraft.

Hold down the Shift key to ensure that the aircraft is sized in proportion and reduce the size by dragging a corner toggle. If you want to change the flight angle at the same time, move the cursor outside of the bounding box and click and rotate the box.

6 Repeat the steps of copying the largest aircraft, adjusting the size and angle in order to create as many different copies as you require.

7 To finish off your creation, you can add a new sky. Using the *Move* tool, drag and drop the sky into the layered stack, and then drag the sky down the layer stack to the bottom, so that it sits beneath all the copied aircraft.

8 If you use the *Eraser* tool on some of the layers that contain aircraft, you can add another dimension, giving the impression of aircraft emerging from the clouds.

COPYING OBJECTS

Replacing a Background

ERASER TOOL

HARD-EDGED BRUSH

EYE DROPPER TOOL

CANVAS SIZE

GRADIENTS

The background to an image can sometimes spoil the total shot. In many circumstances there is little you can do at the taking stage, but plenty you can do back on the computer with Photoshop Elements.

If ever there was a show-stopping color it has to be red. It attracts the viewer's eye into a picture no matter how small a part of the picture it occupies. Despite the eye-catching red in this image, the overall picture needs some work. The setting of a cluttered field is not the best backdrop, so we can remove the car from the field using Photoshop Elements and experiment with some other, more exciting backgrounds.

You can use *Selection* tools to get rid of the background, but using the *Eraser* tool is an option worth exploring.

Open the *Layers* palette from the *Palette Well*, double-click the thumbnail and rename it in the box that appears on screen.

Using the *Zoom* tool, enlarge the car to about 300%; you need it this large to make the eraser cut-out technique easier. Select the *Eraser* from the *Toolbar* and a soft-edged brush about 6 pixels in diameter. With the mode set to *Brush* and the *Opacity* set to 100%, you can begin the erasing.

❷

2 Click down right on the edge of the car with the *Eraser* tool. Hold the Shift key down and move a short distance along the edge of the car and click again. Elements will erase in a straight line between these two points. Because the image is so highly enlarged, you can work around the edge of the car in short steps. Make shorter steps on the curved sections and longer steps on the straighter parts.

3 It will not take you that long to work around the entire car, but keep the Shift key depressed as you work. When you get to the front bumper, you can leave the shadow area between the bumper and the car. That area won't show when you replace the background later. Once you have completely erased around the edge, you can switch to a hard-edged brush and erase the remainder of the background with a larger brush. This is a quick process once the edge of the car has been completed. The red roadster has left that cluttered field and is floating on a transparent background.

4 You now need to create a new background to show the car off. You will also need to create some additional space around it by selecting *Image > Resize > **Canvas Size*** from the *Menu Bar*. Increase the *Canvas Size* a few inches in both the *Width* and *Height* boxes.

❹ Canvas Size

❸

5 Select the *Move* tool from the *Toolbar* and move the car over to the right a little to improve the composition.

6 Open the *Layers* palette, and create a new blank layer by clicking the center icon at the bottom of the *Layers* palette. Click and drag that new layer beneath the car.

7 Select the *Eye Dropper* tool from the *Toolbar* and then click onto an area of dark red color on the car. You will see that you have selected that color and it now appears in your *Color Picker*. We can either use the shortcut keys Alt+ Backspace or select the *Paint Bucket* tool to flood the new layer with red.

8 To add interest to the background, select the *Gradient* tool from the *Toolbar* and black as the foreground color. From the *Gradient* tool *Options Bar*, select the *Linear* option and *Foreground to Transparent* from the drop-down menu.

9 You can now add a *Foreground to Transparent* gradient on the top and bottom of the red background. For more control, apply these gradients to new blank layers. Creating these gradients on new blank layers means that you can make a few dry runs first. You can also adjust them with the *Opacity* slider in the *Layers* palette. To create a gradient, drag out a line that tells Elements where to start and stop the gradient. You can add to the gradient where it needs it with the *Brush* tool.

As all the elements have been applied separately to their own layers within the stack, we are free to experiment. Try other gradients or blend modes.

Retouching Landscapes
Levels and Gradients

Landscape pictures can be disappointing when they are transferred to the computer screen. The drama or serenity that appeared to be there at the taking stage often seem to be lacking when viewed later. You can use Photoshop Elements in a variety of ways to restore the drama to your landscape photography .

1 This picture, taken on the Great Barrier Reef in Australia during a short storm, is an example of drama that has been lost.

2 The most significant change you can make to start this process is with the *Levels* command. Call up the *Levels* command via *Enhance > Adjust Brightness and Contrast > **Levels***, or alternatively use the shortcut Ctrl+L.

3 The image is deficient in both light and dark pixels, as shown by the histogram being peaked in the middle of the histogram box. Drag each of the outer sliders inward toward the edge of the histogram to add highlight and shadow tones, which puts back some of the impact.

4 Adjusting the *Levels* in this way makes a dramatic improvement to the image.

5 The main body of the image has been adjusted, but you can darken the top of the sky to add a little more drama. If you select the *Freehand Lasso* tool from the *Toolbar* you can make an irregular selection of the top part of picture.

Feather Selection

Feather Radius: 100 pixels

OK
Cancel
Help

6 From the *Menu Bar*, choose *Select > Feather* and add a *Feather Radius* of about 100 pixels. This large feather radius will ensure that the extra darkening you give to the top of the sky will be seamless. If you then call up the *Levels* palette again, you can move the center slider to the right until you are satisfied with the darker tones that have been introduced into the sky.

Retouching Landscapes continued
Graduated Filter Effects

Another way to improve a weak sky is to apply a graduated filter effect using a new blank layer and the *Gradient* tools. In conventional photography, a graduated filter is a filter that can be applied to a camera lens. It has a color at the top only, graduating to a clear bottom section. This effect can be created in Photoshop Elements.

1 Create a new blank layer over the top of the landscape and sample a dark tone from the original sky using the *Eye Dropper* tool. A neutral gray from the top right of the picture would seem the best option. That color will appear in the *Color Picker* on the *Toolbar* and we can then click the foreground color to bring the main *Color Picker* on screen.

Elements will already be showing us the color selected, by the position of the small circle over to the left of the palette. If you left-click about one inch below the original color setting you will retain the neutral gray, but darken it considerably.

2 Select the *Gradient* tool from the *Toolbar* and from the options choose *Linear,* then *Foreground to Transparent*. Draw a line down from the top of the image to just above the horizon and the gradient will be formed on the new blank layer.

3 If you wish to reduce the gradient effect, you can reduce the layer opacity from within the *Layers* palette using the slider control. If you want to increase the density of the gradient, you can drag the layer thumbnail down over the copy icon at the base of the layers to double the intensity.

4 You can use these same techniques to add delicate color into your skies in any shade you choose.

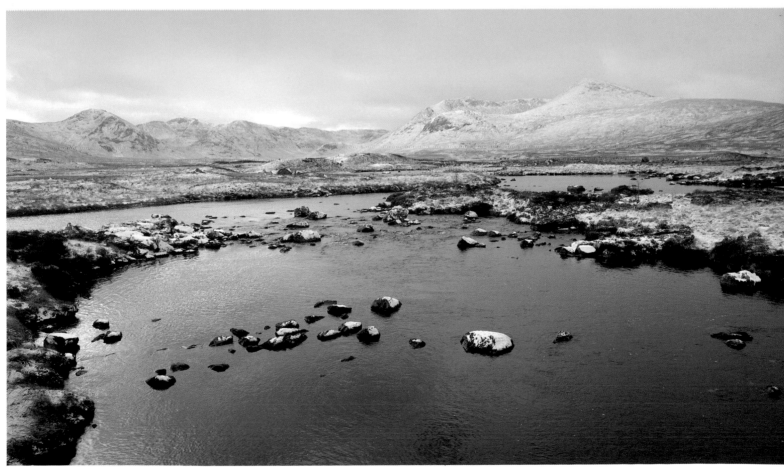

Retouching Landscapes continued
Replacing Skies

There are times when the contrast between the light and dark areas in a landscape is just too high to record correctly; this is true of both images taken with a digital camera and those scanned from film. In these conditions the sky records as white, and this is something that should be altered in order to improve a picture.

1 Your first task is to remove the existing sky; this is not a difficult task. Firstly, click the *Layers* tab from the *Palette Well* and change your background into a layer by double-clicking the thumbnail and renaming it.

2 Select the *Magic Wand* from the *Toolbar* and without any adjustment to the options, click down in the sky area and select it.

3 From the *Menu Bar* choose *Select > Feather* and add a 2 pixel radius.

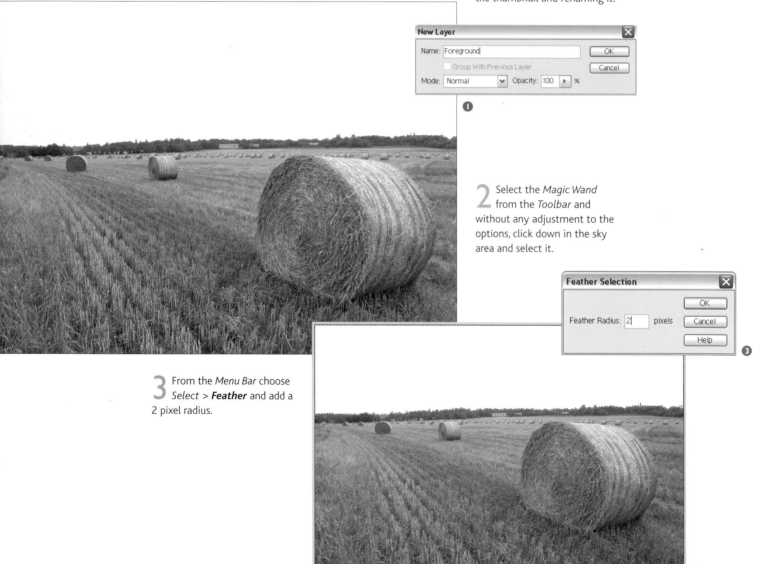

Sometimes when you cut out a light sky to introduce a darker one, the join between the sky and land can look odd. You may get a halo effect as a few light pixels left from the removal of the lighter sky show up against the darker one. To alleviate this, go to the Menu Bar *via* Select > Modify > Expand *and expand your selection by 3 pixels. The expanded selection encroaches into the distant trees by a few pixels, but it won't be noticeable.*

4 Use the shortcut keys Ctrl+X to cut the boring white sky out of the image.

5 You need to select another sky to replace the one removed; a sky taken at the same time as the original landscape is ideal. After taking your landscape image, tilt your camera upward and take some shots of the sky, but with an exposure that allows it to record better.

Retouching Landscapes continued
Replacing Skies continued

6 With your *Move* tool selected from the *Toolbar*, drag the foreground of the landscape onto the sky and, again using the *Move* tool, position it so that it sits correctly in the frame.

6

7 This image would look far better in black and white, so select the foreground layer from the *Layers* palette and click the *Quick Fix* icon on the *Shortcut* bar. Select *Color Correction > **Hue and Saturation*** and move the *Saturation* slider all the way to the left to remove the color.

7

8 Select *Brightness > **Auto Contrast,*** then click *Apply* and then *OK*; the foreground is now monochrome and has an improved level of contrast.

Select your sky layer and repeat the *Color Correction > **Hue and Saturation*** process. If you try the *Auto Contrast* on the sky, the result is likely to be too harsh, so omit that step.

8

9 With the sky still selected in the *Layers* palette, select *Image >
Transform > **Free Transform*** from the *Menu Bar* and Elements
will place a bounding box around the sky layer. Click the bottom
center toggle and move that upward to adjust the perspective of
the sky. This creates a more dramatic, stormy sky effect.

To complete the transform either hit the *Enter* key, click the tick
on the *Options Bar,* or select another tool from the *Toolbar.*

10 Any intrusive areas that remain where the sky meets the
foreground can be dealt with using the *Eraser* tool and a soft
brush on the foreground layer. Save your image as a Photoshop file
retaining the two layers and then flatten the image via *Layers >
Flatten* to add the final touches.

Using the *Dodge* and *Burn* tools, lighten the lines of straw in the
foreground and darken down shadow areas. Finally, use the *Clone*
tool to clone away distracting highlights.

Retouching Landscapes continued
Improving Weather

Photographers will always be at the mercy of poor weather, but we can at least use software to brighten up pictures taken on dull days.

The biggest change you can make to a landscape to give that sunny-day feeling is the inclusion of some blue sky. Landscapes tend to have little tone in the sky on dull days, and clouds are a giveaway that a photo was not shot in sunny conditions. Remove the clouds and you can then add contrast and color using the appropriate Elements tools.

With this image, the clouds are a problem and it is with these that you should start your manipulations.

3

1

1 The clouds in this picture just have to go. From the *Toolbar*, select the *Magic Wand* tool. Using the default setting, click inside the sky; most of the sky will be selected.

Using the *Freehand Lasso* and/or the *Polygonal Lasso* tool from the *Toolbar*, you can add or subtract parts of the selection until the sky is fully selected. Using the *Zoom* tool, enlarge the areas you need to adjust. By holding down the Shift key, you can add to your existing selection made with the *Magic Wand* with any of the other selection tools.

2 In areas where your selection has encroached onto the land, you can hold down the Alt key and remove a part of the selection.

2

3 With the sky fully selected, you can add a 2–3 pixel feather to the selection, then double click the background thumbnail and rename it to change it into a layer. Hit the shortcut keys Ctrl+X and the sky will be removed.

4 Return to the *Layers* palette in order to create a new blank layer and drag that layer down to the bottom of the layer stack. You can then flood that layer with white. Alt+Backspace will flood a layer with your chosen foreground color. This will give you a good base to add a gradient blue sky.

4

5

5 To give yourself ultimate control over the graduated blue color you will add next, create a new blank layer above the white layer. From the *Color Picker*, select an appropriate pale sky blue.

As an alternative, you can try adding some white fluffy clouds back into the sky. Copy a blue cloudy sky into the layered stack above the gradient layer and blend it into the gradient layer using the **Screen Blend** *mode.*

6 Select the *Gradient* tool from the *Toolbar*. From the options, select *Linear* mode and from the edit button, click on *Foreground to Transparent*. Draw a line down from the top of the screen to tell Elements where to start and end the gradient.

6

7 From the *Layers* palette, select the original landscape layer and from the *Menu Bar* select *Enhance > Adjust Color > **Color Variations***. Reduce the *Amount* slider, then lighten the image slightly using the *Lighten* button and add some warm tones with the *Increase Red* button.

8 As a final touch, increase the contrast of the landscape layer via *Enhance > Adjust Brightness/Contrast > **Brightness/Contrast***. Sunlit landscapes naturally have more contrast than a landscape shot under a dull, grey sky.

7

8

Retouching Landscapes continued
Adding Extra Interest

Improving images involves enhancing the good parts of the picture, while subduing or correcting the less appealing parts. Your aim is to attract the viewer to the most interesting parts of the image and then keep them there as long as you can. This project, enhancing a moody landscape shot, is a perfect example.

3 From the *Menu Bar*, choose *Select > Feather* and add a *Feather Radius* of about 25 pixels for a high-resolution image like this. As you add the feather radius the look of your selection will change slightly to reflect the feather.

Before you move onto the next task, hide the selection, but leave it active. It is easier to judge your manipulations with the selection line invisible. Hit the Ctrl+H keys to hide the selection; the same key stroke again will reveal it.

1 Sometimes you can be faced with a charming landscape or waterscape, which only needs something extra to lift it out of the ordinary. This waterscape has just a hint of a sunbeam in the distance, and you can use the tools of Photoshop Elements to enhance this.

You need to carry out the standard remedial work before you start this process, such as adjusting levels and making any color balance changes.

2 Enlarge the image using the *Zoom* tool. With the 10 by 7 inch file at 300ppi, enlarge the section in the sky you want to work on by at least 100%. Working at these magnifications helps you to create seamless manipulations. Mark out the polygonal selection in the place where you want the beam to fall.

4 You will also be able to better evaluate what you are doing if the image is closer to the print size. If you click the *Zoom* tool and the *Fit on Screen* button from the *Options Bar*, the working size will be fine.

From the *Toolbar*, select the *Dodge* tool and from the options at the top of our screen select a brush size that will cover the width of your hidden selection. Select *Highlights* as the *Range* setting and an *Exposure* setting of 2%. You need to be delicate with this process, so 2% is sufficient.

Gently lighten the area to form the beam of light.

⑤

⑥

You can choose to stay with your color image or try some variations such as a monochrome image or a light blue tone via the Hue and Saturation palette.

5 Repeat the process for as many beams as you want to introduce. Vary the width of the beams and the angle.

6 Using the *Dodge* tool, you can now lighten those small light areas of the sky where the beams seem to be coming from. The clouds would be naturally bright at these points but you still need to help them along.

The same techniques can be used to add drama to other images, but a subtle and gradual approach is essential.

TIP

You can make a layer copy of your image before you use the Dodge tool so that from within the Layers palette you can switch between before and after images to judge the tone of the beam. It is easy to overdo this manipulation if you are not careful.

Retouching Landscapes continued
Improving Light

WARM TONES

PAINT BUCKET TOOL

BLEND MODES

ERASER TOOL

MERGE VISIBLE

One thing that affects photographs more than anything else is quality of light. The warm tones of a summer evening can give almost any picture charm.

However, it is not always possible to capture an image in this way. The weather might be against you, but you can help the situation along with your software.

1 From the *Toolbar* select the *Magic Wand* tool. While holding the Alt key, select the entire sky area and feather the edge of the selection by 1 pixel. Change the background thumbnail into a layer by double-clicking it and renaming it in the *New Layer* dialog. You can then hit the shortcut keys of Ctrl+X to remove the sky.

❶

This image was shot in very dull conditions, but at least I managed to capture a good range of tones with which to work. It takes a few stages and manipulations to make the picture look as if it was taken in warm evening light.

2 From the *Menu Bar* you need to create a new blank layer via *Layer > New > Layer*. You can choose a name for the layer; I chose "Color." Click the *Color Picker* and pick a rich warm orange. Now flood the new layer with this color using the *Paint Bucket* tool from the *Toolbar*.

❷

❸

3 From the drop-down blend modes within the *Layers* palette, you need to select *Soft Light*. This will give an all-over warm tone, but it also fills the sky area. If you hold down the Alt key and move the cursor over the dividing line between the upper and lower thumbnail in the *Layers* palette, two linked circles will appear. Click, and Elements will wrap the color around the image and preserve the transparent parts.

4 You need to create the feeling that the low sun is picking out the buildings opposite. From the *Toolbar*, select the *Eraser* tool and a fairly large soft-edged brush. Gently erase the color from the foreground to leave only the buildings and some of the distant boats still colored.

5 You can now save the project in its layered form as a .PSD file and from the *Layers* menu choose *Merge Visible*. The image now needs some attention to the levels. Turn to the *Quick Fix* palette and select *Color Correction > Auto Color*.

4

5

6 If you create a new blank layer and drag that layer to the bottom of the layers stack, you can create a new sky. In this situation the sky is unlikely to be completely blue, so pick a warm tone and a sky blue from the *Color Picker*. From the *Menu Bar*, select *Filters > Render > Clouds* to create a warm evening sky.

6

7

7 You can save the project and flatten the layers together at this stage or you could add a soft focus to add to the feeling of a warm evening light. A slight darkening of the foreground would help too.

Retouching Landscapes continued
Day into Night

Photoshop Elements is a powerful software program, and used carefully it can even turn day into night. As usual, you need to select the right image for this type of treatment as not every picture taken in daylight will react well to this process. This particular shot has a rugged, moody look that works perfectly.

First, add a blue tone to the image via the *Hue and Saturation* palette. You can find this on the *Menu Bar* via *Enhance > Adjust Color > **Hue and Saturation*** or via the shortcut keys Ctrl+U. If you place a tick in the tiny *Colorize* box at the bottom right of the palette, you can then adjust the *Hue and Saturation* sliders to enhance the feeling of night.

2 If you want the night shot to be darker, select the *Levels* command via Ctrl+L and slide the center *Midtone* slider to the right a little.

⋀ *Our example contains scant contrast and a narrow range of tones. In normal circumstances, you could use the* Levels *palette to adjust the levels and transform the image. However, for this technique, you can make use of the tones being flat by turning the daytime image into a nighttime effect.*

3 To take the nighttime conversion one stage further, you can add a light to the lighthouse and a light beam spreading out across the bay. From the *Menu Bar*, create a new blank layer via *Layer > New > **Layer***; you can choose any name in the new layer dialog. You will create your main light on a separate layer so you have complete control over it.

Enlarge the top of the lighthouse using the *Zoom* tool. Then, using the *Polygonal Lasso* tool or the *Rectangular Marquee* tool, make a selection around the area you wish to illuminate. You can then flood the selection with yellow to form the light.

4 Remove the selection via the Ctrl+D keys. From the *Filter* menu select *Blur > **Gaussian Blur*** and from the *Blur* options add about a 5 pixel radius of *Blur* to make the lamp more convincing.

Retouching Landscapes continued
Day into Night continued

5 Although the light looks OK, it is not quite there. Most lamps have a hot spot or bright part, and you can create that on another blank layer. Create the new layer as before, draw an oval selection in the center of the yellow light, and flood that selection with white. Add a little *Gaussian Blur* to the white to form a convincing bulb for the lighthouse.

6 Save the project as a layered .PSD file at this stage. Then you can flatten the three layers ready for the next stage via *Layer > **Flatten***. You now need to create the beam of light, which should be done on a duplicate layer. Select *Layer > **Duplicate Layer*** and Elements will create a duplicate layer. With this duplicate layer selected, use the *Polygonal Lasso* tool to create the shape of a spreading light beam. Feather the edge of the selection by 25 pixels.

7 Call up the *Levels* palette via Ctrl+L and move the center slider left to lighten the selection and create the beam.

8 The new beam works quite well, but it ends too abruptly. You can put that right using the *Eraser* tool from the *Toolbar* with a low *Opacity* setting. Gradually erase the end of the beam from the upper layer. This reveals the layer beneath, which does not contain the beam.

9 The final stage could be to add a *Black to Transparent* gradient to the top of the image. You could also light a couple more windows using the technique already described. Lastly, crop the image and add a few tiny points of light with the *Pencil* tool to create stars in the night sky.

Retouching Portraits
Eyes and Skin

When it comes to improving portraits, you need to be far more critical with your work than you might be with other images. People's faces are so well known that even a slight change can alter their appearance, and a heavily retouched portrait can end up looking fake or "plastic." This will be spotted instantly by the viewer.

Enhancing the eyes

1 First select the *Zoom* tool and enlarge the eyes so they are easier to work on. You will notice that another fault becomes evident—the number of highlights in the eyes.

Deal with those first by using the *Clone* tool. From the *Options Bar*, select a small, soft-edged brush about 8–10 pixels in diameter. Hold down the Alt key and left-click to sample color and texture close to the spot you wish to eradicate. Release the Alt key and apply the sampled pixels over the highlights. As long as you work carefully, there is no need to make a selection first.

With a little care you can erase all the highlights, except the ones that you want.

2 With the image still enlarged, make a selection of the whites of the eye ready to lighten them. You could use the *Magic Wand* tool, but there is a greater need for accuracy with eyes so a better option is to use the *Polygonal Lasso* tool.

Click down right on the edge of the white of the eye and in short steps manually create a selection. If you hold down the shift key, you can make a similar selection of the other eye. It is vital that both eyes are adjusted the same. From the *Menu Bar*, select *Enhance > Adjust Color > Remove Color* or use the shortcut keys Shift+ Ctrl+U. This correction will remove the blue cast from the baby's eyes.

Adjusting the whites of the eye is a task we will need to master particularly with shots of babies. We will often find that they can appear quite gray, especially in their early years. In our picture of Luke this is certainly the case. In fact, the whites of the eye are a soft blue-gray.

TIP

Where you clone from is the most important issue to ensure that the pixels you apply match perfectly. Where you are cloning along edges of pupils or eyelids, you should sample in line with the natural folds of the skin or tones in the eye.

3 From the *Menu Bar*, select the *Levels* palette via *Enhance > Adjust Brightness* and *Contrast > Levels* or press Ctrl+L. You can see the lack of highlights in the flat area to the right of the *Levels* histogram. Move the right slider toward the end of the histogram's downward slope, but take care not to overdo this.

4 While trying to improve images like this, you need to take a step back and look for other areas of the image that are distracting. The bottom corner of this image, for example, cuts right through the baby's hand, which isn't very attractive. You can use the *Clone* tool to clone and follow the fold of the white top.

TIP

Hold down the Ctrl key and press H on the keyboard and the selection will be temporarily hidden. The same key stroke will reveal it again. You will be able to evaluate your manipulations of the eyes better with the selection hidden.

Sharpening the face

1 A baby's picture rarely requires sharpening, as we expect to see a soft skin, but with an adult male portrait the reverse is true.

2 When it comes to sharpening a portrait, you need to be careful not to overdo it. However, with this portrait, it is possible to increase the *Unsharp Mask* settings further than usual, because you expect to see strong, sharp features in a portrait of a young man. You still need to deal with the highlights in the eyes and whiten the eyes if necessary.

From the *Menu Bar*, select *Filter > Sharpen > **Unsharp Mask***. From the *Options*, push the *Radius* slider as far as you can without introducing an unwanted pixel effect.

3 A radius of 1.2 worked best for this image from a 6 megapixel camera.

Retouching Portraits continued
Eyes and Lips

In portrait photography, the eyes and mouth are often the most important aspects of the picture. To improve images, you can lighten and sharpen lips, eyes, and teeth and enhance the color of the lips.

The retouching tools of Photoshop Elements can handle these manipulations without difficulty.

❶

If you look at the mouth greatly enlarged, you will see that there are some highlights on the teeth and gums that need to be dealt with. Using the *Clone* tool with a small soft brush about the same size as the highlight, you can quickly remove these. Afterward, carry on and deal with some of the highlights on the lower lip.

❷

❸

2 You need to sharpen the eyes and possibly the lips in this portrait, but do you need to sharpen the whole image? The rest of the face and the hair look fine. To sharpen just part of an image, you would normally turn to a selection. On this occasion, however, you can create an adjustment layer.

From the *Menu* bar, select *Layer > **Duplicate Layer*** and type a name of your choice in the *Duplicate Layer* box. If you open the *Layers* palette from the tab in the *Palette Well*, you can turn off the new layer you have just created for a moment and select the background layer for this next step.

3 Go to the *Menu Bar* and select *Filters > Sharpen > **Unsharp Mask***. As you are going to sharpen only a few selective parts of the image, you can afford to push a little more sharpness into those areas. You don't need to be too concerned with the detrimental effect of excessive sharpening on smooth tones elsewhere.

TIP

When you need to deal with larger light areas on places like the lips, you can reduce the Opacity *of the* Clone *tool to between 20 and 40% and build up the tone with successive clicks of the* Clone *tool. This is far more forgiving than working with an* Opacity *of 100%.*

4 From the *Layers* palette, select and turn on the duplicate layer you created earlier and select the *Eraser* tool from the *Toolbar*. The duplicate layer is covering the sharpened layer completely, but if you select a soft brush of about the size of the pupil, you can erase the parts of that upper layer that you want sharp —i.e. the eyes and mouth.

This method gives you the best of both worlds, with the sharp parts from the layer below showing through. You need to flatten the two layers together when complete.

5 The teeth also need lightening a little, so select them with the *Magic Wand* tool. Hold the Shift key and click around the teeth until they are selected. From the *Select* menu, add a 3 pixel Feather to the selection and using the shortcut Ctrl+L, open the *Levels* palette. You can lighten the teeth with the center *Midtone* slider, moving it slightly to the left.

6 To adjust the color of the lips you first need to create a new blank layer. Then, from the *Blend* options in the *Layers* palette, select *Color*. You can paint onto the lips any shade of color you want and the lip texture will show through. Why not enhance the subject's natural lip color or go for a more extreme alternative?

Retouching Portraits continued
Skin Tones

Portrait photography, especially if taken inside, is often affected by the colors and tones of the surroundings. Sometimes that will work in your favor, sometimes not. Using Photoshop Elements, you can change the skin tones of your portraits to match what you recall, or, better still, what your sitter would have wanted. In this example, Dawn's skin appears to have taken on a yellow cast where the light was reflected from the wood paneling in the room where the shot was taken.

❶

Start by creating a duplicate layer, via *Layer > **Duplicate Layer***. Enter any name of your choice in the dialog box.

2 From the *Menu Bar*, select *Enhance > **Auto Color Correction*** or use the shortcut Shift+Ctrl+B. Elements does a fairly good job on the image. The yellow color has gone, but the image is now on the blue side, making the skin tones appear too cool.

❷

❸

3 We need a color somewhere between the original image and the adjusted layer.
You can obtain this by opening the *Layers* palette and reducing the *Opacity* of the auto color corrected layer. A 50% *Opacity* blends the two well. You can merge or flatten these two layers together using the command in the *Layers* menu.

4 You can begin the process of enhancing Dawn's complexion by dealing with the shine on her skin. From the *Menu Bar*, select *Layer > New > Layer* and from the *Toolbar* select the *Clone* tool. You are going to clone to a new layer so you don't alter the original image. All the clone work will appear on this new layer until you are happy to combine them later. From the *Clone* tool *Options Bar*, tick the box that says *Use All Layers*.

Your soft-edged brush must be varied in size to suit the area you are working in, and it is best used around a 30–40% *Opacity*. Starting with the forehead greatly enlarged, sample some skin tones that do not show any shine and, using a series of clicks, build up the tone on the new blank layer.

You can extend this method to any lines or wrinkles on the face and around the eyes.

5 The same technique can be applied to remove freckles —in this case on the model's arms. Using the *Clone* tool at 80–100% *Opacity* will deal with freckles very effectively. Remember that you are still cloning to a new blank layer. Turn the layer off from within the *Layers* palette for a moment and look at the difference you have made to the portrait.

TIP

It is usually acceptable to remove lines, moles, and freckles, but be careful with the laughter contours of a face or you may change the person's whole appearance—and not for the better.

6 You now need to carry out the tasks described earlier, such as cloning out highlights in the eyes and lightening the whites of the eyes.

To give Dawn that classic "cover-girl look," you can also add a soft focus (*see pages 54–55*), and then make some fine tweaks of color via the *Color Variations* palette.

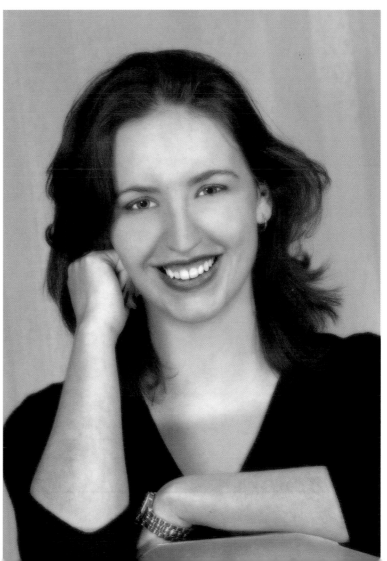

Retouching Portraits continued
Coloring Hair

You can use the tools of Photoshop Elements to change the color of hair as well as eyes. Combine layers, blend modes, and a soft brush, and you can easily brush on a new or different hair color. The same technique can also be usefully employed to remove gray hair. There is no need to stay natural—if you want, you can also experiment with some strange and crazy colors.

1 Start this project by clicking the *Layers* tab from the *Palette Well*, then create a new blank layer by clicking the center icon at the base of the *Layers* palette. From the drop-down blend modes within the *Layers* palette, select *Color*.

With the *Color* blend mode activated, this layer retains any color that you apply without it obscuring the hair texture underneath. As you add the color to a new layer, you can also erase any mistakes without affecting the main image.

2 Select an appropriate color from the *Color Picker*—a dark red, near to brown, is probably the best choice for Dawn's hair. With the image greatly enlarged, apply the color to the new blank layer using a soft-edged brush. As you work around the hair, you can adjust the brush size and the *Opacity* to make the work easier. Use a lower *Opacity* on the edges of the hair and a smaller brush.

3 You do not have to color every individual hair for the transformation to be successful. The more effort you put in, the better the result will be, but the really fine hair on the outer edges needs only a hint of color.

The color you choose for this process needs to be darker than usual because the process has a lightening effect. It may take some trial and error to select the right tone for your subject.

4 If you open the *Layers* palette and temporarily turn off the main picture of Dawn, you will see the hair shape you have created.

Creating the color on a new layer means that you can switch to the *Eraser* tool to remove color from any areas where you have applied too much or the color has spilled over into the background.

5 There is another benefit to working on a new layer. Open the *Layers* palette and drag the hair color layer down over the center copy icon to make a duplicate. Click the *Lock* box at the top left of the *Layers* palette—this restricts any changes that you make to the hair layer to the areas where you have already painted.

Turn off the original hair color layer, select another color from the *Color Picker*, and flood your second hair color layer. Use the shortcut keys of Alt+Backspace to flood the foreground color. The result is an instant hair color change.

Wild styles

Using these techniques, you can change the eye color too to give Dawn a complete new look. You can balance Dawn's hair, eyes, and lipstick, or give her a fun, wild look.

Restoring Old Photographs

It won't be long before you are asked to put your digital skills to work repairing a damaged or faded family picture. When you set out to restore an old or damaged picture, you tend to have scratches and tears to deal with, but how would you deal with a picture that has not only faded badly, but faded to different degrees across various parts of the image?

Photoshop Elements comes to the rescue yet again with the tools to do the job.

TIP

When you are making repairs of this nature, you may not be sure if the color you have chosen is the right one, so try checking with the owner of the picture. Often color will not be that crucial—after all, it's the people in the picture that are most important. However, if you were restoring an image of a wedding dress, for instance, the color may be very important to the bride.

With the old picture on screen, you can see how badly faded it is. Some of that damage can be put right using the Levels palette.

2 To adjust fading, you can use the *Quick Fix* options from the *Shortcut* bar, or you can call up the *Levels* palette using the shortcut keys Ctrl+L. In this case, the *Auto* key did a good job. It has repaired some of the colors in parts of the image, although not the badly faded areas, which will require further attention.

3 You need to work in layers for this repair, so open the *Layers* palette from the *Palette Well* and create a new blank layer by clicking the center icon of the three at the base of the *Layers* palette.

❸

4 You need to apply the correct color to the new blank layer to repair the fading, so the next step is to sample the correct color from the partially corrected image, starting with the background.

Select the *Eye Dropper* tool from the *Toolbar* and left-click within the image to sample the correct color of the background. You will need to make a judgment on where the best color is; in this case it is probably the bottom right of the picture. Once you have sampled that blue color, choose a soft-edged airbrush of about 100 pixels in diameter.

❹

5 Start at the top left corner of the image and spray the blue sampled color into that area. The effect does not look that impressive because the color is covering all the texture in the background.

6 You can fix this by going back to the *Layers* palette. From the drop-down blend mode menu choose *Color*, and, as if by magic, texture will appear in the background. You can continue the task over the whole of the background area. Carefully color the background, taking care around the edges of the other areas of the picture. If you work with the image well enlarged, the procedure is fairly simple.

Once this task is completed, save the image as a Photoshop file and flatten the two layers together via *Layers > **Flatten***. Repair any blemishes or spots on the background using the *Clone* tool from the *Toolbar*.

❺

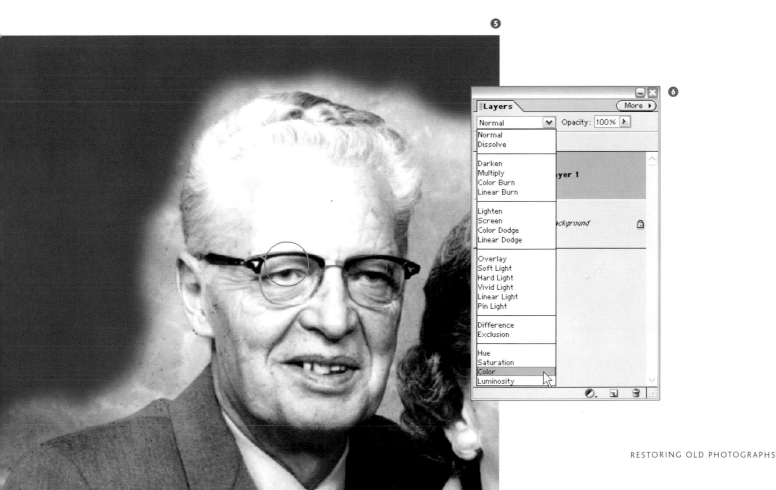

❻

Restoring Old Photographs continued

restoring

7 Repeat the process described in steps 3–6, but this time target the lady's green jacket. Using this method, you can now change the colors you have applied at any time.

8 Open the *Layers* palette and select the color layer that you have already created for the lady's coat. Tick the *Lock* box at the top left of the *Layers* palette. Select a different shade of green, or another color altogether, from the *Color Picker* and hit Alt+Backspace. The color will flood the shape you have created for the coat to produce a complete and instantaneous color change. Once the color shape has been created, changing the color is easy as long as you lock the layer first to preserve its transparency.

9 Save and flatten the image. Repeat steps 3–6, but this time working on the man's jacket. You can work through the remainder of the repairs in the same way.

10 The problem area in this image is the skin tones; it is never easy to get them right and there isn't a good color to sample from in the original picture. Select a pink shade by clicking your foreground color and selecting an appropriate shade from the *Color Picker*. A degree of trial and error is needed. Given the success of the color restoration, this image would be considered a great success by the owners.

Dramatic restorations
The same techniques were used in this example, where the early color tints had faded to the point where the photo could almost be taken as a monochrome shot. Predictably, it was the skin tones that caused the most difficulty, but the end result is still a vast improvement.

TIP

Vary the size of the brush as you work to make your task easier. You can also reduce the Opacity setting of the Airbrush as you work close to the hair and clothes. These options are found at the top of the screen in the Options Bar. If you make a mistake with this color, you can switch to the Eraser, remove it, and do it again.

Fixing Damaged Photographs

One of the most rewarding jobs we can do with Photoshop Elements is to renovate an old photograph. Antique shots are always very interesting, as when we look back at pictures from years ago we get a real sense of the people and places being shown.

Our example was one of a number of old photographs that formed part of a family's collection. The images are fascinating in their own right, even without the personal connection.

The pictures were scanned on a flatbed scanner in the normal way. Flatbed scanners do a great job with prints, but if you want to scan slides or old glass negatives you will need one with a transparency hood.

Renovating an old image is a great way to learn how to use Elements as it requires a number of skills that will be useful when working on other types of image.

It's often difficult to know where to start with renovation work, especially when you look at a section of the photo enlarged. The best way to proceed is by starting with the obvious things first. Once the biggest problems have been sorted out, the rest look less intimidating.

2 A good place to start is with the *Crop* tool from the Toolbar. Don't be keen to crop away too much of the damaged edge of an image, but some of the edge damage can be safely removed.

3 The sky in the image is a fairly uniform gray, so rather than repair the many scratches and blemishes in the sky it is probably best to replace it. Before you start to make any selections of the sky select the *Eye Dropper* from the *Toolbar* and sample two of the gray tones from the old sky before you get rid of it.

Select the darkest gray of the sky you can find as your foreground color with a left mouse click. Hold down the Alt key and click again in the lightest tone of gray just where the sky meets the top of the trees. This will ensure that when we add a new sky it will balance perfectly with the foreground and have the same tones as the one we removed.

The first step in removing the old sky is to select it. In this case, where there's little contrast between the sky and the background, the best tool to use is the *Polygonal Lasso*.

4 Enlarge the image greatly and make a selection around the edge of the sky. As we click down where the sky meets the buildings Elements will anchor the *Polygonal Lasso*. Move an inch or two along the edge and click again. On curved areas, these steps should be shorter, while on straight edges they can be quite long. At first glance this looks a daunting task, but it doesn't take long. Using this method, you can make selections around areas of very fine detail.

TIP

If the selection process goes wrong or you have to leave it part finished you don't have to throw your hard work away. To pick up and add to an existing selection, either hold down the Shift key or click the Add to Selection *icon on the* Options Bar.

5 If you have to save your work for another time, you can save your selection as well. From the *Menu Bar* choose *Select > **Save Selection*** and give the selection a name in the dialog that appears. You can load the selection at any time in the future as long as you save the whole image in a Photoshop .PSD format.

6 When you have completed your selection go to *Select > **Feather*** and add a 2 pixel *Radius* feather. Double-click the Background thumbnail and rename it to turn it into a layer, then choose *Edit > **Cut*** from the *Menu Bar* to completely remove the sky.

7 You can add the new sky right away by clicking the New Blank Layer icon, the middle of the three icons at the bottom of the *Layers* palette. Click and drag the new layer to the bottom of the stack.

Fixing Damaged Photographs continued

8 Select the *Gradient* tool from the *Toolbar*, and then choose *Linear Mode* and *Foreground to Background* from the options. Elements will allow you to draw a line from the top edge of our picture to where the trees meet the checkered background, and this will create a gradient using the two tones of gray you selected earlier. You should save the project and flatten the foreground and sky layers together at this stage.

8

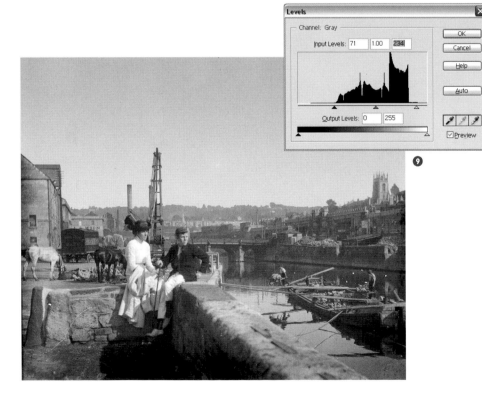

9

9 Select the main image layer and call up the *Levels* palette from the menu via *Enhance > Adjust Brightness and Contrast > Levels*. Move the outer sliders inward toward the edge of the histogram. This adjustment has a significant impact on the image, really bringing the tones to life.

10 At this stage you need to select the *Clone* tool from the *Toolbar* and carefully start to repair the many scratches and marks that cover the picture surface. Given the age of the image it is not really surprising that there is still a fair amount to do.

Hold down the Alt key and Photoshop allows you to sample an area close to a mark, scratch, or blemish. Using a click, move, click motion you can transfer the sampled pixels over the scratch or mark, making a seamless repair.

The cloning task is best done with the image greatly enlarged and you can clone to a new blank layer if you wish. The advantage of working on a new blank layer is that you are never making changes to the original image, which allows you to make good any mistakes easily. Create a new blank layer as you did for the sky and, with the *Clone* tool selected, click the *Use All Layers* box from the *Options Bar*. Any cloning you now do will be to the new layer and not the original.

The cloning task is not difficult, but to get the right result you need to choose your clone source position carefully. For example, if you wish to remove a scratch from brickwork, you must make sure that you clone from an area with similar tones and shades so that the texture of the brick and mortar is retained. With a little care the repair becomes seamless. You can use the same technique to repair a tear or crease in a damaged photo.

Use a soft-edged brush and work around your image repairing the various marks and scratches until you have eliminated as many of them as possible. *Zoom* in close to check your work afterwards.

11 The final task is to sharpen the image. The amount of sharpening you give to an old picture is a personal choice. Use the *Unsharp Mask* filter, but make sure you don't introduce pixellation effect by overdoing it. When finished, save the image then flatten the layers together via *Layer > Flatten*.

It is a good idea at this stage to compare the original with the final image. Bring them both on screen together and select *Window > Images > **Tile*** and both pictures will be placed side by side for comparison. You should see a remarkable change for the better.

Repairing the effects of time
The same methods were used on this antique photo. Clever cropping and tonal adjustment has bought it back to life.

creative
digital imaging

Once you become confident in
your image-editing skills, you will
learn that Photoshop Elements
isn't confined to improving your
photographs. Using layers, filters,
and blend modes, you can also
use it to transform photographs
or parts of photographs into
new and exciting works of art.
From complex montages to
pseudo-watercolor paintings
to attractive pattern pictures
and more, there is almost nothing
you cannot do with the right
technique and a little imagination.
This chapter shares some of the
best techniques—imagination is
one thing that you will have to
provide for yourself.

Flipping Effects

One of the creative ways you can improve your images is by using a flipping technique. This is a simple process, but it can be very effective on the right subject. It is a good idea if you can give some thought to techniques such as these at the shooting stage. While digital-imaging techniques are good and can correct many of the faults introduced during the shooting of a picture, it is best to be aware of what you intend to do at the taking stage.

1 Open up the *Layers* palette from the *Palette Well* and rename the background to convert it into a layer. Double-click the thumbnail to bring up the *New Layer* dialog.

2 You need to create canvas space for the flipping technique. To do that, go to the *Menu Bar* and select *Image > Resize > **Canvas Size***. Clicking in one of the nine squares at the base of this palette anchors the image to that side or corner—pick the middle-right square for this image. You need to double the width of the canvas, but if you overdo it you can always crop back to size later.

This image was taken with the flipping technique in mind. I framed up the shot as best as I could so it would make half the picture.

3 You now have the space to create a mirror image of the picture. This will occupy the blank left half of the canvas.

4 Open the *Layers* palette and drag the thumbnail down the *Layers* palette and drop it on the center copy icon at the bottom. Elements will create a duplicate layer. You can rename it, if you wish, by right-clicking the thumbnail.

From the *Menu Bar*, select *Image > Rotate > **Flip Layer Horizontal*** and Elements will create the mirror image. Use the *Move* tool from the top right of the *Toolbar* to move the left half of the image into place. The image now looks a little squat, but you can fix that by adding some width to the image. Save your work as a Photoshop .PSD file before moving on.

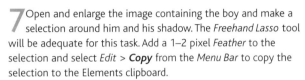

5 From the *Menu Bar*, select *Layers* > **Merge Visible** and Elements will join the two layers together. Select *Image* > *Resize* > **Image Size** from the *Menu Bar* and you can add some width to the image without affecting the height. You can do this by ticking the *Resample Image* box and by removing the tick in the *Constrain Proportions* box. Highlight the width and type in a new width setting.

6 Our image needs a focal point and what better than a person on the pier. The boy was taken from another photo taken in a similar position on the same day. This makes it easier to merge into the image.

TIP

Holding down the Ctrl key will turn any tool you have selected into the Move tool. Release the Ctrl key and the original tool returns. This is a useful shortcut when you are moving and arranging objects in the picture space.

7 Open and enlarge the image containing the boy and make a selection around him and his shadow. The *Freehand Lasso* tool will be adequate for this task. Add a 1–2 pixel *Feather* to the selection and select *Edit* > **Copy** from the *Menu Bar* to copy the selection to the Elements clipboard.

Click out of that image and back into the original one and select *Edit* > **Paste** from the *Menu Bar*. Elements will paste the selection into the layers stack. You can then use the *Move* tool to move the boy into place. Use the *Free Transform* tool to reduce his size if he looks out of scale with the environment.

You can use the flipping technique in other ways. Here I copied the landscape, then flipped it vertically to create a basic "reflection."

Action and Movement

Capturing movement in pictures at the taking stage demands some simple skills like panning with a moving subject. The background will blur, leaving the subject crisply focused. That's the theory, anyway, even if things don't always work out as you would wish!

You can improve your pictures by adding action and movement using the tools of Photoshop Elements; one of the most effective is *Radial Blur* from the *Filters* menu. This effect is similar to the zoomed effect created by zooming a telephoto lens during an exposure.

∧ *This image was shot in very bright conditions, and the feeling of movement has not been captured as well as it could have been. Using Elements tools can introduce some action.*

1 This shot will be improved by the application of the *Radial Blur* filter, but not if you apply it to the image as a whole. The surfer—the center of interest—would be lost if you did.

Select the *Freehand Lasso* tool from the *Toolbar*. Your selection does not need to be precise and will take only seconds to do. Just follow the rough shape of the surfer and his surfboard.

2 From the *Menu Bar*, choose *Select > Feather*. For this task you need a high feather value of at least 100 pixels. The selection is currently covering the center of the image, but you need the center protected and the edges selected. Do that by choosing *Inverse* from the *Menu Bar*, or use the shortcut Ctrl+Shift+I.

3 Go to the *Menu Bar* again via *Filters > Blur > Radial Blur* and Elements will present you with the *Radial Blur* dialog. For this technique, select *Zoom* as the *Blur Method*.

Choose *Draft* from the *Quality* setting. This seems to give a more gritty and attractive zoom effect. The *Zoom* amount is a personal choice and you can try out a few different settings. Here, I used a setting of 40.

2

3

Radial Blur

Amount 40

OK

Cancel

Blur Center

Blur Method:
○ Spin
⊙ Zoom

Quality:
⊙ Draft
○ Good
○ Best

4 ❹ If you click into the thumbnail on this palette, you can drag the *Zoom* effect and place the center of it roughly over the center of interest on the picture, which is the surfer. Click *OK* and Elements will do its work. Hit Ctrl+D to remove the selection and evaluate your work.

❺

5 To enhance the overall effect of the picture, you can also darken the outer edges a little. Make a freehand selection around the outer edge in a rough oval shape and then inverse the selection. Add a 150 pixel *Radius* and using the *Levels* palette (Ctrl+L) move the center *Midtone* slider to improve the impact.

TIP

Use the Draft *setting to see a quick preview before running* Radial Blur *at* Best. *The filter can be slow to run at* Best, *so experiment in* Draft *then redo it.*

Layers

Normal ▾ Opacity: 100% ▸

Lock: ☐ 🔒

Eagle

Sky

∨ *With the sky layer selected, you can introduce a* Motion Blur. *You must ensure that the angle of the blur matches the bird's flight.* Motion Blur *can also be applied to the eagle layer via a feathered selection. If you make a feathered selection of the back of the bird, it will ensure that the head, eyes, and beak remain sharp.*

∨ *Another advantage of having each part of the image on a separate layer is that it gives you the ability to change the composition by moving the bird.*

∧ *In the second example, you can again use the* Blur *tools, but this time the* Motion Blur *filter. Cut the eagle out from its original background and make sure that both it and the sky sit on separate layers.*

Color to Black and White

Light rarely gives the correct exposure or contrast for all the different tones in our pictures, making most exposures a compromise. How many times do you have a great sky and almost black foreground or a great foreground and a white sky?

Here, we are going to reduce a color image to monochrome and adjust the various tones so that the end result has a crisp black-and-white sparkle.

2 Begin by making tone and contrast adjustments to different parts of the image. This usually entails selections, but not in this case. Start by getting some balance between the darker foreground and the lighter distance.

Open the *Layers* palette from the *Palette Well*. Click the *New Adjustment Layer* icon at the bottom left of the *Layers* palette, and then the *Brightness and Contrast* option.

1 You can convert the image to monochrome in a number of ways, but the quickest method is to use the shortcut Shift+Ctrl+U.

With an adjustment layer, you are not changing any of the tones in the original image, only on the adjustment layer. Click the Layers *tab in the* Palette Well *and you will see the adjustment layer and the mask that Elements attaches.*

3 You need to introduce more contrast to the central part of the water in the image. Move the Contrast slider slowly upward, concentrating on getting the tones right in the area you want to affect. Ignore the effect that this manipulation may have on the sky and the rest of the image, as you can deal with that next.

4 You can now use the adjustment layer to balance the tones. Select black as the foreground color and the *Linear Gradient* tool from the *Toolbar*. Set the *Gradient* options to *Foreground to Transparent*. Draw a line down the image, extending from the top of the sky to about two-thirds of the way down. Elements will apply a gradient to the adjustment layer and mask the sky. You now have a beautiful blend of the top and bottom tones.

5 These manipulations still leave the immediate foreground stones a bit dark, so let's deal with these next. Open the *Layers* palette and select the original landscape at the bottom layer of the stack, then make a simple *Freehand Lasso* selection of the foreground. From the *Select* menu, choose the *Feather* command and add a 100 pixel *Feather* to the selection. This ensures that changes you make in the foreground will blend well into the middle distance.

6 Call up the *Levels* command via the shortcut Ctrl+L and adjust the sliders to lighten the foreground tones. You can do the same thing to the sky by making a quick, irregular-shaped *Freehand Lasso* selection first.

7 Adjusting the tones and contrast separately in different parts of the image has made quite a difference.

You can also clone out the distracting white building on the other side of the water and then flatten the image using the *Layers* > **Flatten** command.

8 The sky top right is a little weak in tone. This can be adjusted with another adjustment layer or a freehand selection. Lastly, you can add some *Unsharp Mask* to sharpen the image, then compare it with the original shot.

The changes that have been made to different parts of the image have made good the camera's compromise exposure. This image has been adjusted using both selections and an adjustment layer, but you can decide which way of working you prefer.

Toning

Using the tools of Photoshop Elements you can apply many toning effects, which, providing they are used correctly, can alter the mood of your pictures and improve them immensely.

The important part of toning is to select the right pictures to apply the tones. That is not to say you cannot apply any tone to any image, but some tones will definitely seem more appropriate than others.

In this example image, the original color does not add much to the picture. The fact that this is a very old cottage means that it lends itself very well to sepia toning.

1 There are many ways to create a sepia tone. You could use the *Quick Fix* tools, but the best option is found in the *Menu Bar*. Select *Enhance > Adjust Color > **Hue and Saturation*** or use the shortcut Ctrl+U to bring up the *Hue and Saturation* palette.

To begin the sepia tone process, tick the *Colorize* box at the bottom right of the *Hue and Saturation* palette. The whole tone of the image should change instantly.

2 You can now adjust the *Hue*, *Saturation* and *Lightness* sliders to achieve the sepia tone. Apply a setting of 25 as the *Hue* value and 10 for the *Saturation* value to start with. These settings will create a sepia tone, but further adjustments to the sliders allow you to create just the right depth and color.

This image, scanned from a 35mm monochrome negative, is an excellent choice for a sepia tone. The settings used for the cottage work equally well for this old shot of an early car.

Another favorite tone is a blue tone. It is created in exactly the same way, but with a slight change of settings. A Hue value of 215 and a Saturation value of 25 creates a pleasingly serene shade of blue. This winter landscape lends itself especially well to the treatment.

This toning technique can be used more creatively by combining several tones in one image. The background sky in this example was toned by making a selection with the Magic Wand tool and feathering the edge of that selection by a pixel value of around 25–30. The Feather command is found via Select > **Feather**. The Magic Wand picks up only part of the sky, allowing you to tone that area. You can then repeat the process on different parts of the sky, introducing a different tone with every selection.

Each time you carry out this process, you will get a different effect depending on what the Magic Wand automatically selects.

Spot Color

Using an adjustment layer is a great way to color your images selectively to bring out interest or detail in them. Having made one, you can use a brush to select which parts of the image it will or will not affect. Here we use this method to add a sepia tone to an image, then reveal the green flag and the red of the guard's buttonhole.

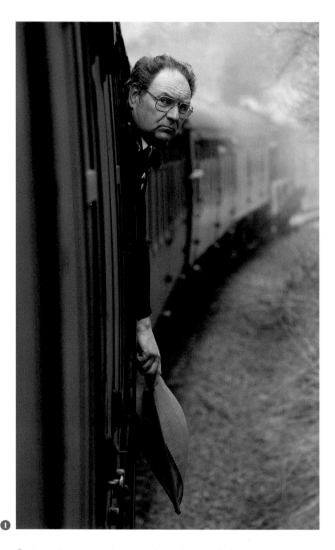

1 Open the *Layers* palette via the *Palette Well*, then create a new adjustment layer by clicking the icon at the bottom left of the *Layers* palette, or by selecting *Layer* > **New Adjustment Layer**.

2 Either way you will be presented with a list of possible adjustment layers. Go down to the third section and choose *Hue and Saturation* from the options.

First of all, click the *Colorize* box in the *Hue and Saturation* palette, then move the sliders until the saturation reads about 10 and the hue 25. If you want to save time or be exact with your settings, you can ignore the sliders and type the numbers directly into the boxes above.

3 As seen in the previous tutorial, this procedure produces a good sepia tone. When you are completely satisfied with the shade and depth tone, click *OK*.

TIP

Use the square bracket keys immediately to the right of the P key to scroll up and down brush sizes quickly and easily.

4 One of the advantages of working with an adjustment layer is that at any time while you are working on an image, you can double-click the adjustment layer thumbnail on the *Layers* palette and the *Hue and Saturation* palette will open.

An adjustment layer can also be saved and brought back into play at a later date, as long as you save the file as a Photoshop .PSD file.

5 To bring back the original green of the flag, first enlarge the image until the flag in the guard's hand fills the screen; it is much easier to mask the flag at this size. Select a soft-edged brush and choose black as the foreground color. You can then carefully spray black onto the sepia flag and the original green will begin to show through. Using varying brush sizes and a varying *Opacity* setting we can reveal the green flag from the layer beneath.

If you make an error while spraying black onto the adjustment layer, change the foreground color to white and repair the overspill. White applies the adjustment, black removes it.

5

6 Finally, use the black paint to reveal the red of the carnation on the guard's lapel.

You can use this adjustment layer trick in many different settings. In this second example there was no real center of interest until I reduced the whole image to monochrome and revealed just three people at the table in color.

6

Hand Tinting

Have you ever wondered why children's coloring books are so addictive? Many adults can't resist the temptation to pick one up and try doing it themselves—when no-one is watching, of course. It's therapeutic and satisfying, and perhaps that's why hand-tinting images is so much fun; for a short while, you can become an artist.

The tinting process works better and looks more attractive with delicate colors, so pick an image that will lend itself to such treatment. Here, I chose a close-up of a piece of rock.

1 You will need to add your color onto a new blank layer. Go to the *Menu Bar*, select *Layer > New > **Layer*** and in the box that appears type "Color" as the layer name.

2 You need to change the blend mode from within the *Layers* palette so that, as you apply color, the texture of the rock shows through. Click the *Layers* tab from the *Palette Well* and select *Color* from the drop-down menu.

3 Next, choose a color to work with from the *Color Picker* palette. It is best to stay with delicate tones for this technique.

4 Select the paint brush from the *Toolbar* and an *Opacity* setting of about 10% from the *Options Bar*. Use a soft-edged brush at about 100 pixels diameter. You will need to vary the diameter of the brush as you work so that you can keep your color within the sections of the rock.

5 To apply the color, carefully paint inside one of the rock sections on the new blank *Color* blend layer.

6 Select other colors from the *Color Picker* and paint in other sections of the rock's surface.

One of the rock shapes you can leave blank in order to insert a picture into that space. You can then create the illusion that you have painted that picture too.

7 With the lighthouse image on screen, select the *Move* tool from the *Toolbar* and drag and drop the lighthouse into the rock picture. Call up the *Transform* tool using the shortcut Ctrl+T and, while holding the Shift key, drag a corner toggle to size the image to fit this section of the rock.

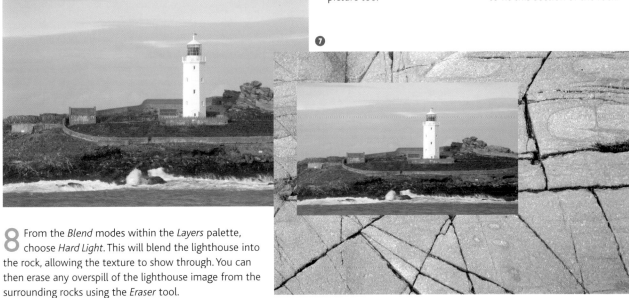

8 From the *Blend* modes within the *Layers* palette, choose *Hard Light*. This will blend the lighthouse into the rock, allowing the texture to show through. You can then erase any overspill of the lighthouse image from the surrounding rocks using the *Eraser* tool.

Vignetting

When a good shot is spoiled by distractions at the sides or corners of the image, there are several approaches you can take. Cropping can eliminate the problem, or you can clone out those ugly dark corners. A vignette, however, not only adds charm to a portrait, it also covers up the offending areas.

When taking pictures of pets, it is important to get down to their level. That is what I did with this example picture of Skipper. The close-up nature of the image has given it impact, but there are some distractions around the edge of the image that need to be dealt with. The vignette approach would be perfect for this example.

2 You can create a vignette directly onto the image on screen, but that limits your control of the vignette. A better way of working is to use a new blank layer. Go to the *Palette Well*, click the *Layers* tab and then click the central icon of the three at the bottom of the *Layers* palette to create a new blank layer.

TIP

You can rename any layer by right-clicking the thumbnail and typing a name in the new layer box.

3 Select the *Elliptical Marquee* tool from the *Toolbar* and draw out an oval shape, centrally placed over the picture, starting in the top left corner. This selection will allow you to make changes only to the central area of the picture, so switch the selection to the outer edges via the shortcut Shift+Ctrl+I.

4 To create an effective vignette, you need to feather the edge of the selection via *Select > **Feather*** from the *Menu Bar*. Choose a high *Feather Radius* of about 100 pixels to obtain a soft, graduated edge to the vignette.

With white selected as the foreground color, hit Alt+Backspace or use the *Paint Bucket* tool from the *Toolbar* to flood the oval shape with white. Remove the selection via Ctrl+D and you have your vignette.

5 It is a good idea to add 1–2 pixels of monochrome *Noise* to any computer-generated color that you add to an image. While this is almost undetectable on screen, the smooth tones of computer color can look a little plastic when printed. Go to *Filter > Noise > Add Noise*. The palette that appears on screen may seem to be blank, but Elements has just drawn the information for the thumbnail from the center of the screen, which in this case is transparent. Click and drag the thumbnail to the left or right and the vignette will come into view.

6 Sometimes you will want to increase the intensity of the vignette. Click and drag the vignette layer down the *Layers* palette and drop it over the center *Copy* icon. This creates a duplicate of the vignette layer and the intensity of the feathered edge is intensified.

Creating the vignette on a separate layer allows you to adjust the vignette easily using the Opacity *slider in the* Layers *palette. Although this vignette works well with the example image at 100% Opacity, you will sometimes need to reduce the intensity of the vignette for a better result.*

Vignettes don't have to be white; black can be more appropriate as long as it is in keeping with the image. The selection also doesn't have to be an oval or elliptical shape. With this picture, the selection was made via the Freehand Lasso *tool. As the image had a much higher resolution, the* Feather Radius *needed to be increased to 200 pixels.*

Once you have flooded the selection and removed it via Ctrl+D, you can add to the vignette with the Brush *tools if necessary. Almost any color can be used for a vignette—the important thing is that your choice balances well with the image.*

Aging Effects

Whenever you attempt to change the mood of an image, your first consideration should be selecting the right image. It is important to apply the right techniques to the right picture.

This is true of many digital techniques, and the addition of filters is one example. If you select the wrong image with the wrong effect you are unlikely to improve your images very much.

Creating aged effects can add something to an image. Old pictures generally have a certain charm, and you can create and convey that to a viewer.

The aim is not to be deceitful and trick the viewer, but to create an effect without destroying the appeal of the picture. This is rarely a one-click process, and you may have to make several manipulations to achieve the desired effect.

This image was carefully selected to ensure that it would react well to an aging-effect technique. A sepia tone is often associated with an aged image so try that first.

1 Using the shortcut Ctrl+U, call up the *Hue and Saturation* palette and tick the *Colorize* box down on the bottom right of the palette. For a sepia tone, the *Hue* setting needs to be around 25–30 and the *Saturation* around 10. As aged pictures are often faded, you can also adjust the *Lightness* slider a little to simulate that effect.

2 You can use the *Craquelure* filter from the *Texture* menu to break up the surface of the image. However, this filter does not work very well on high-resolution images and, as this image came from a 6 megapixel camera, the resolution needs to be reduced to get a reasonable result. This is not a problem as you are deliberately reducing the image quality for effect anyway.

3 You can then run the *Craquelure* filter, found via *Filters > Textures > Craquelure*.

4 You can also apply a ragged-edge effect by using the *Wet Media Brushes*. To find these, first select the *Brush* tool from the *Toolbar*, then go to the *Options Bar* and click the small black triangle alongside the brush shapes. Select *Wet Media Brushes* from the palette.

5 Select brush number 8 and white as the foreground color, then manually create an irregular border around the image.

Take time to experiment with the image. You may want to make use of the Dust and Scratches *filter from the* Noise *menu along with the* Craquelure *filter and other brushes to create an irregular effect.*

If you go outside of the Elements effects to third-party filters such as Dreamsuite Photographic Edges, you can find specialized filters, such as Mud Cracks, *which also create an aged effect. Other filters within the Dreamsuite package even create the effect of tape stuck onto the picture's surface.*

Painterly Effects

Almost all image-editing software comes with effects filters that are fun to try out, and Photoshop Elements is no exception. As well as the filters that are a part of Elements, you can add more filters made by other software developers. These filters are usually installed into the plug-ins folder within the Photoshop Elements program structure. As you load up Elements, it reads the third-party filters and adds them to your filter list.

Adding filter effects to images is great fun, but they can become tedious if you overuse them. Filter effects are easy to apply and are often used on the wrong image to cover up mistakes and errors. To work well, filter effects need to be used sparingly and on the right choice of picture.

To really get people's attention, you need to avoid using the same old filters and create something different that cannot be obtained by a single click of a button. This technique came from Barry Colquhoun, who kindly shared it with me. It involves a blend of four layers and filter effects, but is simple and easy to do.

The technique does not work so well on images with fine detail or those with large expanses of even tone such as a blue sky. Good choices are images that fall somewhere in between, like the one shown here.

Your filter choices within Elements can be accessed in two ways. You can click the Filters tab from the Palette Well and access your filters via the thumbnails. This method will give you some idea of what effect that particular filter will apply. Click the thumbnail and the options for that filter will be presented to you. If you already know which filter you wish to use, you can go direct to Filters from the Menu Bar and just pick your choice from the menu.

With all filters, the effect varies depending on the resolution of the image. Filters work on pixels, so more pixels means the effect is less pronounced. Therefore, if you don't get the result you want first time, reduce the resolution of your image and try again.

1 For this filter process, you need to make a number of layer copies. From the *Menu Bar* select *Layer > Duplicate Layer* to make a layer copy. In the new layer box, type the name "Filter Layer." Repeat this process to create a third layer copy and title this "Color Layer." Repeat again and call the fourth layer "Opacity Layer." These names reflect the process you are going to apply to each layer.

Click the *Layers* tab from the *Palette Well* and you will see the four layers. The bottom layer, or background, is going to sit there just as insurance. This is advisable as filter processes sometimes affect parts of the image a little too much. Keeping an intact original means that you can start afresh if you have to.

2 For the moment we need to turn off the top two layers and the Background by clicking the eye icon. The layer we need to start our filter process is the second layer, the one that we called "Filter Layer" in step 1.

3 Start by selecting *Filter > Artistic >* **Plastic Wrap** from the *Menu Bar* and the options for this filter will appear on screen. In most cases the default settings work fine, so stay with those, at least to start with, and click *OK*.

4 The result that appears on screen after the filter has run is not that attractive, but don't abandon it just yet. Go back to the *Filters* menu for the next stage via *Filters > Artistic >* **Cut-out**. Again the default settings of 4, 4, and 2 will work well. Apply the *Cut-out* filter to the same layer as the *Plastic Wrap* filter.

5 The result still doesn't look that impressive, and it has lost a lot of color as well. This will be addressed later, but for now, save your work and move on.

6 Turn to the "Color Layer" to correct that loss of color. Open the *Layers* palette and select the "Color Layer" by clicking into the thumbnail; the layer will become selected ready for editing. This will hide the filtered layer below. The next step is to blend the "Color Layer" with the one below using blend modes.

Go to the blend modes drop-down in the Layers palette and select *Color*. Elements will now blend the color of this layer with the filtered layer below.

Painterly Effects continued

7 The image will now have a lot more color and appeal. With just the "Filter Layer" and the "Color Layer" turned on, select *Merge Visible* via *Layers > Merge Visible* from the *Menu Bar*. Photoshop will merge these layers together ready for the next stage.

8 Now turn on the "Opacity Layer." Using the *Opacity* slider, you need to allow a little of the original image to blend with the filtered part. Reduce the *Opacity* to zero then slowly move the slider back up the scale to get just the right balance between the filtered and the unfiltered layer.

9 You can merge these two layers together once you are happy with your blend. This leaves you with just two layers; Background and the "Opacity Layer." Take a moment to consider what else needs to be done to achieve a really good result. With this technique, a lot depends on the image used.

10 Here the filter effect has not been very kind on the two faces. You can correct that using the Background (insurance) layer. Turn on the Background layer by clicking the eye icon, but select the "Opacity Layer" for editing.

Using the *Eraser* tool, gently remove the filtered detail from the upper layer to reveal the unfiltered faces from the layer below. You need the image well enlarged to make this task easier. Then, from the *Layers* menu, select *Flatten* and Elements will convert the remaining two layers to one.

11 From the *Menu Bar* select *Image > Adjustments > Levels* or use the shortcut Ctrl+L. Move the outer sliders inward toward the edge of the histogram to add more contrast to the image.

12 Next, go to the *Menu Bar* and *Filters > Sharpen > Unsharp Mask*. With this effect, you can afford to be a bit heavier with the sharpening settings than usual.

13 Finally, call up the *Hue and Saturation* palette via *Enhance > Adjust Color > **Hue and Saturation*** or use the shortcut Ctrl+U. This process can often stand a little more color *Saturation* than usual. Here, +20 *Saturation* was added for the final result.

Painterly Effects continued
Watercolor

While the artistic filters seem to be the natural choice if you are trying to recreate a painted style in Photoshop Elements, they aren't the only choice or necessarily the best choice. Alternative filters, or even combinations of filters, can sometimes produce more effective results, as you can see from this example.

This image was shot with a 3 megapixel camera. Its clear lines and bright colors are perfect for an artistic treatment.

To start the filter process, make a duplicate layer in the same way as before.

2 From the *Menu Bar* select *Filter > Blur > **Smart Blur*** and the options for this filter appear. From the *Quality* option select *High* and from the *Mode* option *Edge Only*. The *Radius* and *Threshold* sliders enable you to create more or fewer edge lines, but for this image leave them at the default setting. Click *OK* and Elements will create white lines on a black background.

3 You actually need black lines on a white background for this technique. This is simply achieved via *Image > Adjustments > **Invert*** or via the shortcut Ctrl+I.

4

4 Click the *Layers* tab again from the *Palette Well* and from the drop-down *Blend* modes select *Soft Light*. This will give the image a watercolor effect as the lined layer is blended with the original layer in the layer stack.

5 From within the *Layers* palette, click into the original layer at the bottom of your layers stack to select it for editing. From the *Menu Bar* select *Filters > Pixelate > **Crystallize*** and choose a *Cell Size* of about 20. You then need to soften the edges of those "crystalized" shapes to create more of a watercolor effect. Do that via *Filters > Blur > **Gaussian Blur***, adding a 5 pixel *Radius* blur.

5

6 The layer blend process you have used has caused the tones in the combined layers to be a little weak, but that works in your favor to give the image a convincing watercolor effect. Now flatten the layers by selecting *Layer > **Flatten Image***.

6

Adding Texture

Adding texture to digital images may seem an odd thing to do. It involves taking images, often from high-quality cameras and lenses, and then degrading the quality of the image with the application of a filter.

So, why would you do it? Because, on the right subject, it adds to the charm of the picture and helps to improve it. As with filters, textures should be used sparingly and with an appropriate image.

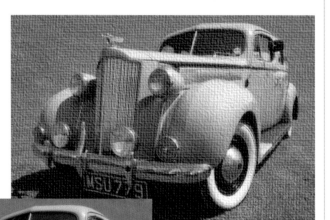

The resolution of an image affects how the texture will appear. In this example, the same image is shown with the same texture applied using exactly the same options. However, one image is 300ppi and the other is 72ppi. Both images are 10 by 7 inches, and you can clearly see that the lower-resolution image shows the effect of the texture far more clearly. If they were both printed at this size, the texture in the 72ppi version might seem heavy and clumsy, while the higher-resolution image would not show the effect very much at all. In fact, it might even look like an error rather than an attempt to improve the image.

To apply textures, you need to select the right image. This shot has already been treated with a watercolor effect, so using an appropriate texture will add something worthwhile to it. This image is 10 inches on the long side and has a resolution of 300ppi.

2 Select textures by clicking the *Filters* tab from the *Palette Well* and choosing a filter via the thumbnails. If you double-click the *Texturizer* thumbnail, the *Options* palette opens up. Clicking on the *Texture* drop-down menu enables you to take a look through all the options you have at your disposal.

TIP

Rule one has to be to save your image without a texture before proceeding any further. It is always good practice to save your images with and without a texture. You never know when you may want to use your image without the texture and you cannot remove one at a later date.

3 You can also click the plus or minus icons below the thumbnail to adjust the image/thumbnail size so that it matches the print size of the image. This helps you to evaluate the scale and relief of your texture.

Choose the *Burlap* texture and adjust the scale and relief settings. For a high-resolution image such as this a high setting will generally be required in the scaling slider. A low-relief setting generally works best for many of the *Texture* tools.

4 Adjust the *Light Direction* and you will see the effect of your choice in the thumbnail. Click *OK* and you can appraise the image on screen at the print size. At this stage you can still use the *Undo History* if you feel that the settings are not quite right and want to run them again.

TIP

Always evaluate the effect of any texture you place on your image at the size you intend to print the image. Select the Zoom *tool from the* Toolbar, *then click* Print Size *on the* Options Bar. *Textures that look fine on screen can look too heavy in print.*

ADDING TEXTURE

Adding Texture continued

Additional textures

This second example is another image that lends itself well to a texture effect. With the image on screen, choose *Filter > Texture > **Texturizer*** from the *Menu Bar* and from that drop-down menu select *Load Texture*.

There are some other texture effects that come with Photoshop Elements and you need to locate them after selecting *Load Texture*. From the *Look In* drop-down box, look in the folder where Photoshop Elements has installed itself on your hard drive, and find a folder called Presets. This contains additional textures.

2 Select *Frosted Glass*; this is a larger-scale texture that works better with higher-resolution images.

Each texture will have a different effect on your images, so experimentation is the key. That is why you should always save a copy of the original, untextured image in a safe place before starting.

Combining textures

We can also include more than one texture on our image if we wish.

In our example we can add a coarser texture to the outer edge of our image and a finer one on the inside. This is best accomplished with a selection.

2 There are two approaches we can take here. We could use the *Lasso* tool from the *Toolbar* to create this selection freehand if we wish. Otherwise, we could use the *Elliptical Marquee* tool to create a more uniform selection.

3 Before we apply any texture effects we need to *Feather* our selection to ensure a gentle blend between the two texture effects. On this 5 megapixel image a feather *Radius* of about 150 pixels will give us the result we need. Find the *Feather* command in the *Select* menu and experiment until you get the right setting.

4 From the filter menu we can now select the texture effect we require for the center of our image. *Frosted Glass* is one of those textures that can be found in the Elements Presets folder, as described on the opposite page.

TIP

It can be a bit of a journey to find these filters, so it is a good idea to locate the folder and copy it to a more convenient place on your hard disk.

5 To add a texture to the outer edge of the image we must first inverse our selection via *Select > Inverse* or via the shortcut Ctrl+Shift+I. We can then choose another texture effect like Rust Flakes to complete the effect. Not all combinations work well together, so use a bit of trial and error to find something that works on your image.

6 As usual with Photoshop Elements, only our imagination limits what we can achieve with our software.

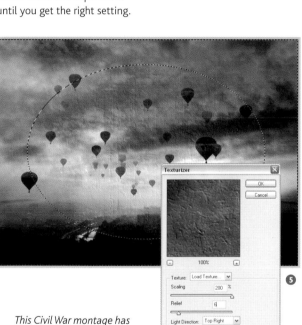

This Civil War montage has been filtered with the Rust Flakes *texture found from the* Load Texture *option.*

Other Effects and Filters

Adding filter effects to your images often gets the thumbs down, but that doesn't have to be the case if they are used carefully and on the right subjects.

The first thing to remember with all filter effects is that the effect will vary slightly depending on the resolution of the image. Filters are fun and experimentation is the key. The worst that can happen is that you have to hit the *Undo* key. You can never be entirely sure what effect a filter will have on an image until you try it out. Some filters can be used straight from the *Filter* menu onto an image and will work well, but others will not.

This example shows one of the filters applied straight from the Elements Filter palette. The image is bold with little fussy detail; this type of picture lends itself well to the Cut-out filter.

Rough Pastels *is another filter that tends to work well on bold images. Even the introduction of monochrome* Noise *to an image can add some appeal. To improve an image you often need to temper the effect with other techniques. Filters are never a surefire cure for a poor image by themselves.*

Sketch filter

1 This image of a mountain cottage is a good example of where using layers can help an effect. Click the *Layers* tab from the *Palette Well* and create a duplicate layer. The quickest way is to click and drag the thumbnail down the *Layers* palette and drop it over the center icon at the base.

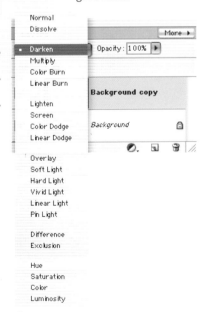

2 Select *Filters > Sketch >* **Note Paper** from the *Menu Bar* and the options for the filter will open up. You can now increase the *Image Balance* slider to create the effect— somewhere around 45 gives a good result.

3 The effect doesn't look very impressive yet, but try blending the layer with the original layer below. Open the *Layers* palette and select *Darken* from the drop-down blend modes.

4 The result is an image that appears with just parts of the image in relief. The effect looks particularly attractive when printed onto matte paper.

Other Effects and Filters continued

GLOWING EDGES

DIFFUSE GLOW

DRY BRUSH FILTER

EDGE BRIGHTNESS

SMOOTHNESS

Colored Pencil filter

This lighthouse picture is an image from a 3 megapixel camera. As before, you need to make a layer copy of the original image before applying any filters.

2 Selecting the *Eye Dropper* tool from the *Toolbar* allows you to sample colors from within the picture. I selected two shades of blue from the distant hills. With the *Eye Dropper* tool, a left-click selects the foreground color; hold the Alt key and click again to select the background color. The *Colored Pencil* filter makes use of the colors in the *Color Picker* when it processes the image.

3 Select *Filters > Artistic > Colored Pencil* from the *Menu Bar* or from the *Filters* tab in the *Palette Well*. Run the filter with the *Paper Brightness* set around 39. You can then use the *Eraser* tool to remove some of the filtered layer to reveal more of the original lighthouse layer below. You can decide just how much of the filter effect you want and where you want it to show.

4 You can then flatten the image from the *Layers* menu and add a *Texture* filter to complete the work.

Diffuse Glow filter

1 Start the filter process by making a duplicate layer from the *Layers* menu.

2 From the *Menu Bar* select *Filters > Distort > **Diffuse Glow*** and adjust the settings to 8 for *Graininess*, 12 for *Glow*, and 3 for *Clear*, then click *OK*.

3 The filter process loses some detail in the sky and at the top of the building, so use the *Eraser* tool to erase some pixels from the *Diffuse Glow* layer to reveal these parts of the original layer beneath.

4 You can choose to present the image in color or remove the color and present it as a monochrome image. To remove the color, select *Enhance > Adjust Color > **Hue and Saturation***. Alternatively, use the shortcut Shift+Ctrl+U.

Other Effects and Filters continued

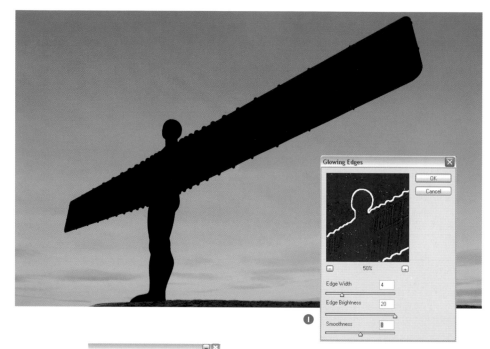

①

Glowing Edges filter

You see a lot of images where the Glowing Edges *filter has been applied, and they all tend to look much the same. You can use your software and apply some creativity to come up with something more imaginative. This is an image of the huge English metal sculpture, the Angel of the North.*

1 Start this technique by creating a layer copy, as you have with the other filter examples. Then select *Filters > Stylize > Glowing Edges* from the *Menu Bar*. The options for this filter are a personal choice, but I chose an *Edge Width* of 4, an *Edge Brightness* of 20, and a *Smoothness* of 8.

②

2 Once you have run the filter, choose *Overlay* from the *Layers* blend modes. This picks out the *Angel of the North* with a white line, and gives the sky an unusual and attractive appearance.

Dry Brush filter

One of the most attractive filters is the Dry Brush *filter from the* Artistic *group. This filter is more affected by image resolution than* Glowing Edges, *so this image was reduced to a 72dpi file of around 2.7 megabytes.*

Make that all-important layer copy and select *Filters > Artistic > **Dry Brush***. The default settings work just about right for this image.

2 The *Dry Brush* filter adds an attractive look to the image, but as often happens, it also obliterates some of the finer detail. You can fix that using the *Eraser* tool. Select a soft-edged brush around 40 pixels in diameter and erase some of the filtered layer over the cottage and boathouse. I included the landing stage to the left in this step, because there was some nice detail there that had been lost with the addition of the filter.

Digital Respray

Have you ever wished your car was a different color, but been put off by the cost and hard work of spraying it? Well, you can now respray it digitally using Photoshop Elements. Not only will it save you a fortune in paint and body shop charges, it could also save you from an embarrassing lapse of good taste.

The first task is to remove the background to make a transparency. To do this you can use either the *Polygonal Lasso* tool or the *Selection* brush.

This image has a bit of a color cast, but this can be removed by hitting the shortcut keys for desaturate: Ctrl+Shift +U. You also need to change the Background into a layer by double-clicking the thumbnail to rename it.

2 Using the *Zoom* tool, enlarge the image to somewhere around 300–400%. This makes it is easier to make the selection. Click down on the edge of the car and Elements will anchor the *Polygonal Lasso* tool. Move a short distance and click again. Make short steps on curves and longer steps on the straighter edges.

3 From the *Menu Bar* go to *Select > Feather* and add a 1 pixel *Feather* to the selection.

4 Inverse the selection via the shortcut Shift+Ctrl+I. Elements will switch the selection so that the entire background is now selected. Choose *Edit > Cut* from the *Menu Bar* or hit the shortcut Ctrl+X to cut away the background. This leaves the car floating on a transparent base, and you can repeat this process for the areas inside the windows.

Go up to the the *Menu Bar* and select *Layer > New > Layer*. You can enter any name in the new layer box that appears. Pick a mid-blue from the *Color Picker* and flood the new blank layer using the *Paint Bucket* tool.

5 The result doesn't look that good yet. The car is blocked out on the layer beneath by the blue layer. Open the *Layers* palette and hold down the Alt key. Move the cursor over the dividing line between the top and bottom layer and the cursor will change to two linked circles. Click and Elements will wrap the color around the car shape.

6 Open the *Layers* palette again and reduce the *Opacity* of the blue layer to 70% using the slider at the top right of the palette. From within the *Layers* palette, select the *Soft Light* blend mode from the drop-down menu. The car now looks as if it has been resprayed. However, the "painter" hasn't masked off all the chrome parts or the wheels. These areas will be fixed next.

7 Select the *Eraser* tool from the *Toolbar* and a soft-edged brush. You need to erase color from the color layer in areas of the car that don't require any color. Once you have completed that, you can create another new blank layer for the background. Drag that layer to the bottom of the stack and flood it with black using the *Paint Bucket* tool.

All the hard work is now done, so make sure you save your project as a Photoshop .PSD file. You have given the car a convincing respray. Why not use another image in place of the colored layer next time? The effects can be quite striking if you use a flower, for example.

DIGITAL RESPRAY

Adding Type

Creating text and text effects using Photoshop Elements can be purely functional—to title an image, for example—or it can be much more inventive. You can even use text interwoven with an image.

When text is created, Elements places it on a new layer, so you can import previously created text into another image by dragging and dropping the layer in the same way as you would for any layered composition.

2 Select the standard *Horizontal Type* tool and click into the picture space. You will be presented with a flashing cursor of the sort you might see in a word processor. If you look at the *Options Bar* at the top of the screen, many of the choices may also look familiar. These include *Font*, *Font Size*, *Font Color*, *Bold*, *Center Text*, *Left Align Text,* and so on.

1 Go to *File* > **New** from the *Menu Bar* and you will be presented with an *Options* palette. You can choose a custom size for your new page or select one of the many options from the drop-down menu. The other options are pretty standard and include *Background Color* and *Mode*. Most of the time you are likely to be working in RGB and the background color can be your own preference. You also have the option to work in transparent mode.

With the new page created, select the *Type* tool. This is represented by the letter T on the *Toolbar*. There are four options grouped together, including *Horizontal* and *Vertical Type* and *Horizontal* and *Vertical Type Mask* tools.

3 Click in the *Text Color* box, select *Black* and type the word "Size" on screen. The word is likely to be fairly small. Highlight the text and increase the type to 72pt. This is as large as the standard text sizes go.

4 You can in fact make the text much bigger than the 72pt maximum value that appears in the drop-down menu. Highlight the text value on the *Options Bar* and type in any value of your choice.

You can reselect the *Type* tool at any time and highlight the text to change all or any of the options available from the *Options Bar*. The text remains live and editable all the time.

3 Size

4 Size

The Beauty of Landscape

1 Photoshop Elements can be used to make a slideshow (*see pages 196–97*). For now, let's create a title for a slideshow of our images. You need to create a new document as you did earlier and decide on the title text. If you choose a title such as "The Beauty of Landscape" you can create each word on a separate layer if you wish. This is not essential, but it does give you far more control over where the words appear on the page.

Select the font and font size and after typing each word click the tick on the *Options Bar*. Each time you will need to click back into the image to get the type cursor to appear before typing the next word.

2 If you open the *Layers* palette from the *Palette Well*, you will see that each word is located on a separate layer and that each layer has been given a title. You can select each layer and adjust or move each word around the picture space.

3 You can now click into each layer and adjust the text to a pleasing design, varying the font sizes and position until you arrive at an attractive layout.

4 If you highlight the word "Landscape" and click the *Create Warped Text* icon from the *Options Bar*, many more text effects open up. Choose *Flag* and, using the sliders, adjust the amount of distortion you want in the text.

If you save your text image as a Photoshop file, you can return to it at any time and the text will remain live—i.e. you can highlight and change it in any way you choose.

A subtle green color might be more suitable for the title of a landscape slideshow, so you could simply highlight the text and change the color.

5 If you want to move all four words around the page together you need to link them. If you turn off the background layer and select one of the word layers, you can link them by clicking the small square to the right of the *Eye* icon. A small linked chain icon appears. You can then move all the text layers together with the *Move* tool. This linking works with the other tools of Elements as well, such as the *Transform* tools.

The Beauty of Landscape

The Beauty of Landscape

The Beauty of Landscape

The Beauty of Landscape

Adding Type continued

TEXT STYLES

DROP SHADOWS

BEVEL EFFECT

CHROME SETTINGS

STYLE SETTINGS

You can create some far better text styles using the Layer Styles *palette. Many variations and options open up if you click the* Layer Styles *tab from the Palette Well.*

With the "Landscape" layer selected, you can click into any of the thumbnail options such as the Drop Shadows *and your shadow choice will be created on the text. To remove the shadow or any other effect, click the* Clear Style *icon at the top right of the* Styles *palette.*

If you experiment with these options you will find that you can add more than one style to the text. Here, both a Drop Shadow *and a* Bevel *effect have been used.*

To adjust any of these settings, you can open the Layers *palette and double-click the* Layer Style *icon to the right of the thumbnail. Elements will open up the* Style Settings *dialog and you can adjust the effect.*

TIP

From the drop-down menu inside the Layer Styles *palette, you can view a substantial collection of effects and styles at the click of a button. To check out many of the layer styles on the text, it helps to have all the words on one layer, but you sacrifice some flexibility when you merge them all together. To avoid doing so, try this tip:*

Create a new blank layer at the top of the layer stack and turn off the white background layer. With the blank layer selected and the word layers turned on, hold down the Alt key and from the options in the Layers *palette select* Merge Visible. *Elements will merge the four layers of text together in the new layer, but will leave the originals intact.*

Take time to experiment with the huge choice of effects on offer. The Chrome settings look very realistic and some of the styles under the Complex heading are interesting.

While you are having all this fun in the Layer Styles palette, do not lose sight of what you want the title for. A set of landscape slides probably demands a subtle title. Do not forget that even at this stage you can still alter your original text. The layer styles will update to match your changes.

If you want to add other effects to your live text such as erasing an area of it, you need to right-click the thumbnail layer and select Simplify Layer before applying the Eraser or one of the other tools.

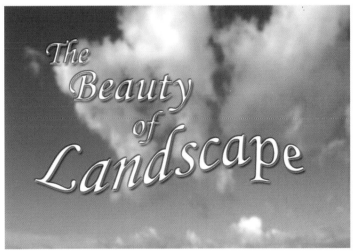

If the basic later styles are not enough, you can select Text Effects from the Effects tab and apply one of those options.

Photographic Text

The *Text* tools within Photoshop Elements along with the *Layer* styles give you a fair degree of creative freedom, but you can also make text from your own images.

The text you create should be appropriate for the purpose. An example would be a series of images on the theme of "water"—what would be more fitting than to make your text from an image of water?

2 Click and hold the *Type* tool icon from the *Tool* bar and select the *Horizontal Type Mask* tool from the options that roll out. Click within the picture space and you can then type your chosen text. You will see the majority of the image masked, apart from the text.

3 Highlight the masked text to make changes to the font and font size and warp the text from the icon on the *Options* bar in the same way as standard text. When you are happy with your text, click the tick on the *Options* bar and Elements will create the text as a selection.

1 In this example, text was created from an image of reflections in the water of a harbor. Before you begin to create your text, you should carry out the usual remedial work on the image such as adjusting levels and correcting color. You should also change the background into a layer by double-clicking the layer thumbnail and then renaming it.

4 If you select any of the *Selection* tools from the *Tool* bar, you can drag the text selection around the image to place it just where you want it. You can also save any selection you make for later use. From the *Menu* bar choose *Select >* **Save Selection** and type a name into the box provided.

Your selection will then be saved with your image as long as you save the image as a Photoshop file. You can then retrieve it at any time via *Select* > **Load Selection**.

5 Add 1 pixel of *Feather* to the text selection and then cut and paste the selection to a new layer. To do this you can select *Edit* > **Cut** and then *Edit* > **Paste**. If you look into the *Layers* palette, you will see the two layers. Turn off the original layer and the "Water" text made from the image of water can be seen.

6 You can now use either of the two layers to create some eye-catching text. First, you need to create a new blank layer, flood that with white, and drag it to the bottom of the layered stack. With a white background you will be able to see more clearly the text effects you are creating.

7 With just the background turned on and the Water text selected you can add some interest to the text.

8 With just a couple of clicks from within the *Layer Styles* palette you can add an interesting *Bevel* and a *Drop Shadow* that will bring the text alive.

9 If you turn off the water text layer and select the original water layer, you can apply layer styles to that too. If you apply an inner shadow you can create the effect of lifting the word "Water" above the water image.

Often the least complicated effects work best—this example was produced from a simple shot of the sky.

10 If you apply a low drop shadow, we appear to be looking through a cut-out beneath the water layer. Alternatively, use both layers, increase the saturation of the text even more and apply a filter to the whole—the *Median* filter was used here.

Adding Shapes

Occasionally you will want to add some graphic shapes to your projects, particularly CD covers, business cards, and letterheads. Photoshop Elements provides many such shapes for you to choose from. The *Shape* tool on the *Toolbar* has a number of options grouped with it; just click and hold and they will all roll out.

1 To create shapes, you need to create a new document by selecting *File > **New***.

2 You can select any layer by clicking into the layer thumbnail, which then allows you to edit the shape. You can change to a different color simply by selecting a new foreground color and flooding the color into the shape. You can use the *Paint Bucket* tool for this task or the shortcuts Alt+Backspace and Ctrl+Backspace.

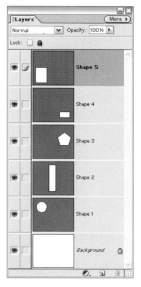

◁ *Once a* Shape *tool has been selected the specific options for that tool will appear in the* Options Bar.

3 Click the *Show Bounding Box* option from the *Options Bar* and select a layer. Click into the shape on that layer and you can alter the size and shape by dragging the toggles around the edge of the bounding box. You can then commit that new shape by clicking the tick on the *Options Bar*. Hold the Shift key while dragging a toggle and the shapes will retain their original shape and only the size will change. If you drag the toggle without holding Shift you will also alter the shape.

∨ ＞ *The* Shape *tool works in a similar fashion to the* Text *tool in that every shape you draw will fill with your foreground color. The shapes will also appear on their own separate layers, as you can see if you open the* Layers *palette by clicking on the tab in the* Palette Well.

4 Select a layer and click the *Simplify* button on the *Options Bar*. The shape then becomes a transparency with the familiar checkerboard effect.

There are other options for use with the *Shape* tools. With the *Square* and *Oval* shape tools, you can select the pixel radius from the *Options Bar*. If you select the *Polygon* tool the option becomes a choice of how many sides you want the shape to have.

There are just too many shapes to list, and each can be drawn out in several ways, from long and thin to short and fat.

5 If you select the *Custom Shape* tool from the options, a myriad of choices appear. Click the small black triangle icon at the top right of this palette and many more shapes open up.

2 You need to prepare the photographic part of the project. In this case, the model needs to be separated from the background. Use the *Eraser* tool to accomplish this to get a gentle blend around the hair. Select the *Move* tool from the *Toolbar* and have both your shape and your photographic image on screen. Click into the photographic image and drag and drop it into the shape layer. You also need to place Dawn behind the shape. Do this by changing the stacking order. Drag the photographic layer beneath the shape.

Adding shapes to photos

I You can not only add layer styles to your shapes, as you did with your text, but you can also add shapes to your photographic subjects.

Create a new canvas that is a similar size and resolution to the image you wish to use. You can then draw out the shape of your choice and add an attractive style from the *Layer Styles* palette.

3 Using the *Eraser* tool, you can now erase parts of the shape to create the impression that Dawn is entwined with it. Finally, experiment with backgrounds to find something that will complement the image.

Creating Line Work

A huge variety of clip art is available for use in all sorts of projects, such as word documents, letterheads and business cards. Some of it is good, some of it is bad, but most of it is generic and not particularly distinctive. Why bother with it at all, when you can create your own line work or clip art from photos with Photoshop Elements?

Line work with Smart Blur

1 From the *Menu Bar*, select *Filters > Blur > Smart Blur*. In the drop-down *Quality* box on the *Smart Blur* palette, select *High*, and then choose *Edge Only* from the *Mode* box.

The slider setting will vary depending on the image you have chosen, so you have to experiment to get the right effect. However, the default setting can be remarkably close.

Sometimes when you create line work from photographs the filter can create too many lines, making the result fussy. You can control the lines that are created by adding a tiny amount of Gaussian Blur. You only need 1–2 pixels of blur to take a little of the sharpness off the image.

2 Your line art will appear as white lines on a black background, but you can reverse that easily from the *Menu Bar*. Select *Image > Adjustments > Invert* or use the shortcut keys of Ctrl+I.

TIP

If you need to make the lines a little thicker you can do so via the Menu Bar. *Select* Filters > Artistic > **Poster Edges** *and the lines will thicken slightly.*

3 Now select a hard-edged brush from the *Toolbar*. With white as the foreground color and the *Opacity* set at 100%, you can touch up your line art, getting rid of lines that are not needed.

Here, I removed the mooring ropes and some of the pier on the upper right. If your line art is to be used on a business card or letterhead, you may need some room for text.

Combining line art

As with your other creations, you can combine line art works in a single image. This "hand-drawn" seagull was created in the same way as the boat on the opposite page.

Before you drag and drop it into the layer stack, you must remove all of the white background so that only the seagull shape remains. Rename the seagull background to change it into a layer, then double-click it and add a name in the New Layer box.

If you select the *Magic Wand* tool from the *Toolbar* and untick the *Contiguous* box, all the black edges of the gull will be selected as you click on a line. Inverse the selection via the shortcut Ctrl+Shift+I, so that the selection is now picking out the background.

In some cases you want your line art completely isolated. In the previous example, the boat dock scene would very likely need a black line around the edge. This piece of line art, however, could be transported into almost any document.

2 Select *Edit > **Cut*** from the *Menu Bar* and your seagull will now be sitting on its own transparent background.

3 With the *Move* tool selected, drag the gull into the sailboat line art. Using the *Transform* tools, you can size the gull and position it where you want it.

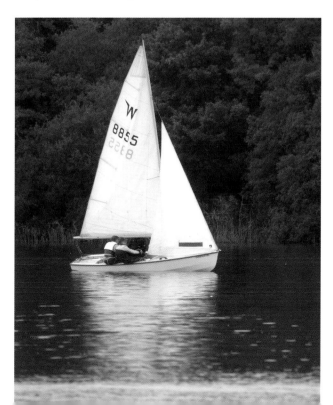

Making Montages

Montage images can be great fun to produce. They consist of two or more pictures fused together to create something unique—an image that could not be created at the touch of a button. Montages can be as fantastic or as realistic as you like. The key thing is to make your images blend together as seamlessly as possible.

This is an example of a two-image montage, in which the Stars and Stripes is introduced into an image of a bald eagle.

❶

I The first task is to remove the blue background from our eagle image. This can be accomplished by selecting the *Magic Wand* tool from the *Toolbar*. Click down into the blue background around the eagle with the *Tolerance* option set at the default setting of 32. Elements will select some of the background, but not all of it.

4 Now select *Edit > **Cut*** from the *Menu Bar* or use the shortcut keys of Ctrl+X. The checkerboard effect tells you that the background has been removed and the area is now transparent. This is a good time to save your project as a Photoshop .PSD file.

2 Hold down the Shift key and you can add to a selection. Click down elsewhere in the blue background and with a few clicks you can have all the background selected.

3 From the *Menu Bar* choose *Select > **Feather*** and add a 2 pixel *Feather* to your selection. This is necessary to prevent the edges of your cut from being too sharp. Click the *Layers* tab from the *Palette Well* and double-click the eagle thumbnail. From the *New Layer* palette rename your background layer using a name of your choice.

❷

❹

New Layer ❸

Name:	Bald Eagle		OK
	☐ Group With Previous Layer		Cancel
Mode:	Normal	Opacity: 100 ▸ %	

5 With the eagle transparency and the Stars and Stripes on screen select the *Move* tool, click into the eagle image and drag and drop it onto the Stars and Stripes. While your *Move* tool is still selected, drag the eagle into place to the right of your image space.

6 Click the *Layers* tab from the *Palette Well* and you will see your two-layered montage.

9 With the flag on a separate layer to the eagle you can, if you wish, select *Gaussian Blur* from the *Filters* menu and add a 15 pixel *Blur Radius* to make the eagle stand out even more. Save the picture as a Photoshop .PSD file. This will retain the layers. You can flatten the image from the *Menu Bar* via *Layers > Flatten*.

7 The image looks pretty good, but you could use your *Transform* tools to extend the flag upward to lose the unsightly folds at the top of the flag. Click the *Layers* tab from the *Palette Well* and click into the flag or background layer to make it ready for editing. From the *Menu Bar* select *Image > Transform > Free Transform* and a small dialog box appears. This dialog box indicates how well Elements has been programmed. It knows that you cannot transform the background and offers to change it into a layer for you. Click *OK* and the *New Layer* dialog appears. Enter a name, then click *OK* again.

8 Elements will then place a bounding box around your flag layer. You need to click the center toggle at the top and drag the bounding box, stretching the flag upward. Click the tick on the *Options Bar* when the procedure is complete.

Making Montages continued
Multi-image Montages

It sounds obvious, but the first thing to consider when putting together a number of images to create a montage is where to start. A good idea is to select a base shot on which to overlay other images.

Three key factors to creating a successful montage are: good color balance between the images you use; good composition (which you will have to create as you build your montage); and a good subject. Color balance can be adjusted much later in the creation process once you have assembled all the components of the montage.

It is unlikely that you will have an exact mental picture of how your final montage will look before you start. Montages tend to evolve and you have to be prepared to import other images into your montage and be ready to change those that don't work. Images from a steam railroad were chosen for this example; all these various images are of the same place and were shot at the same time.

The starting image already has a good composition; it also helps that the focal point of the image is a person. As you overlay images onto this one, you can build on the strength of that composition.

1 Open the second image and using the *Move* tool, drag and drop that second image into your background to make a second layer.

2 The train then needs to be reduced in size. It might also help if you get rid of it before starting any blending. You can get rid of that white sky easily using the *Magic Wand* tool. Click into the sky and Photoshop will select it for you. Feather the edge of the selection by 2–3 pixels using the *Feather* palette from the select menu. Choose *Edit > Cut* from the *Menu Bar* to action the removal. If you click the eye on the background layer, you will see that all the sky has gone. The squares tell you the area is transparent.

❸

❹

3 You need to resize the steam train by selecting *Image >
Transform > Free Transform* from the *Menu Bar* (Ctrl+T).
Photoshop will place a bounding box around your image. While
holding down the Shift key to ensure that your size remains in
proportion, drag a corner toggle to the size you require.

4 Save your project as a
Photoshop file at this stage
and call it something like
"Project 1." Select the *Eraser*
tool from the *Toolbar* and a
soft-edged brush of between
100–200 pixels in diameter
from the *Options Bar*.

❻

5 Set the *Opacity* of the
Eraser to no more than
20% and gradually erase
unwanted detail on the steam
engine layer, blending it
gradually into the image below.
How much you erase is a
personal choice, but stay on the
safe side as you can always
return to this layer later and
erase a little more. Save your
work again at this stage and
call it "Project 2."

❺

6 You need to import your third image of the brass nameplate
into the montage in the same drag and drop way we used
earlier. Use the *Transform* tools (Ctrl+T) as before to size and
position the nameplate. Then select *Hard Light* from the drop-down
Blend menu in the *Layers* palette. This *Hard Light* blend process will
help the nameplate to blend into the other two layers. You can help
that further using the *Eraser* as before.

Making Montages continued

SOFT LIGHT BLEND

HARD LIGHT BLEND

SATURATION

BURN TOOL

HIGHLIGHTS

TIP

The Hard Light *or* Soft Light *blend modes can work well with these types of images, but also consider the* Opacity *slider in the* Layers *palette—it will allow you to reduce the opacity of any layer to any degree.*

7 The process from here is a repeat of what you have already done, but you can experiment with blend modes and layer opacity, finishing off the blends with the *Eraser*. Save your project often so that you can return to a previous state at any time.

Add the white dial to your layered stack, resize it and, after choosing *Hard Light* use the *Eraser* again and blend the edges into the montage. Save your project after each addition. Repeat this with the other nameplate. *Hard Light* won't help here, so use your *Eraser* tool to blend it fully into the image. Add the remaining brass image in the same way as before. When you are happy with the montage, save it in its layered form as a Photoshop file and choose *Layer >* **Flatten Image** from the *Menu Bar*.

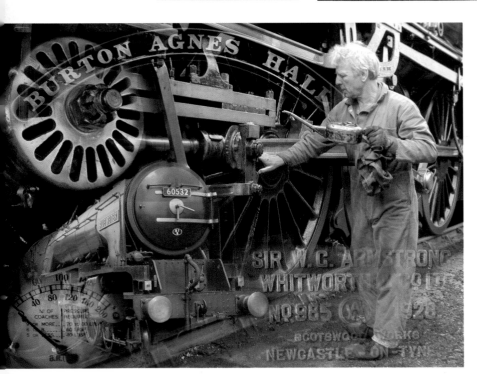

TIP

When you have the Free Transform *bounding box surrounding an element of your montage, you can click inside it and drag it around, or move outside the box and click to rotate your layer. Take some time to experiment with the position and attitude of each element—that's what montage is all about!*

159

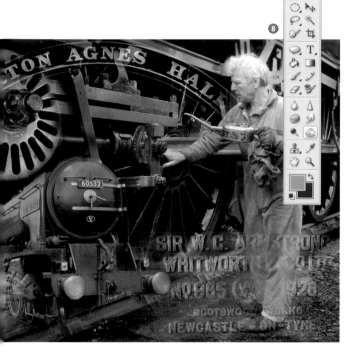

8 You now need to deal with all the unwanted highlights in the image. You can use the *Burn* tool for this process. Go to the *Option Bar* and select a very low *Exposure* of around 5%. Choose a soft-edged brush and set your range to *Highlights* before working your way around the image, darkening down all the unwanted and distracting light parts.

TIP

You can go back to each layer at any time and adjust the size of each image. This is important because you will often find it necessary to make changes as the montage develops into a finished image.

9 You can now try a few experiments with color balance. Open the *Hue and Saturation* palette from the *Menu Bar* via *Enhance > Adjust Color > **Hue and Saturation*** and tick the *Colorize* box. Adjust the sliders for a pleasing sepia tone or perhaps a blue tone. Try using a new adjustment layer to add an all-over tone with just a hint of the original color coming through.

Making Panoramas

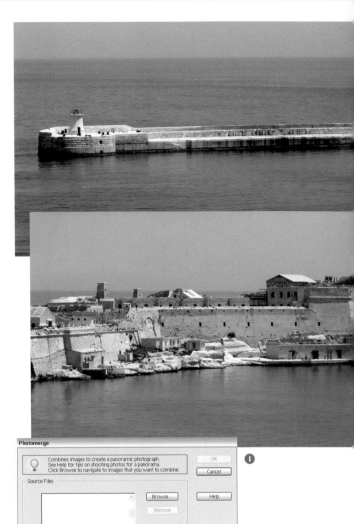

Panoramic pictures, which use two or more images displayed together, have always been a popular way to present those pictures that clearly benefit from that treatment. Seascapes and landscapes are among those that immediately spring to mind.

You can display your panoramic pictures in several ways. You can produce each part as a separate image and place them together in an irregular way; these are often called "joiner" pictures.

You can also blend each image together so that the resulting panorama is completely seamless and appears as one long image. These images do not display at their best on computer screens because the restriction of width means the images must be quite small. However, printed out at full size they can be dramatic. If you place six images side by side, for example, the result may be a panoramic image around five feet long.

Photoshop Elements comes complete with the tools you need to produce these panoramic images, but this is one area where you should consider the *Photomerge* process at the time you take your pictures.

Ideally, you should shoot your panoramic images from a steady tripod that is set up as level as possible. You should also allow a 50% overlap between the images you take, so that your software has a better chance of blending the images together seamlessly. It is also good practice to switch the controls of your camera to a manual exposure setting and take all the shots using that one exposure. Select a white balance that fits the scene, such as "cloudy" or "sun" and avoid taking the pictures on an auto setting.

These measures will ensure that the images you produce have a better chance of being blended together perfectly via *Photomerge*. Having given that advice, the pictures here were all taken hand-held with none of the compensations mentioned above. They were originally taken for use in a joiner-style panorama, but they also demonstrate the power of Elements, in that although the images are not perfect, a superb end result was achieved.

1 From the *Menu Bar*, select *File* > **Create Photomerge**. This brings up the *Photomerge* palette. The palette gives you advice on what to do next via a text panel in the center. The advice at this stage is to click the *Browse* button to locate your images.

2 Our examples are a series of six images that were shot on the island of Malta. I allowed some overlap of each picture as I took it, but not the recommended 50%. Highlight the files and click open to start the procedure.

3

3 All the files will then appear in the *Photomerge* palette. The text panel in the palette explains what it is going to do and even tells you where you can find shooting tips.

4 Click *OK* and wait (it takes a short while to perform this procedure). When the results of the engine room appear on screen, you may notice some slight weaknesses in the blends. As the images were not shot with this process in mind this is not surprising.

You can see some banding on the example panorama, but nothing that you cannot deal with. At this stage, the panorama is likely to be so long on screen that you may need to scroll from side to side to see the whole length.

5 To the right of the *Photomerge* palette, you can see some options, including an *Advanced Blending* option. Tick the *Advanced Blending* box and then the *Preview* button. Click *OK* and Elements deals with the problem. Within a few seconds the banding is almost entirely gone.

4

TIP

When using the **Clone** *tool to reduce banding (see Step 7, overleaf) drop the* **Opacity of the Clone** *tool to about 40% for seamless results.*

5

Making Panoramas continued

6 With Advanced Blending completed, you can review the Photomerge. Select the *Zoom* tool from the *Toolbar* and click the *Fit on Screen* button from the *Options Bar*.

7 You can now select the *Crop* tool and crop the image into the panoramic shape. As you drag out the crop shape over the image, you will notice that to crop effectively you will leave a blank area. This is because the original pictures were not taken on a tripod. However, you can use the *Clone* tool to fill in those areas of sky or water. Any slight banding that shows can also be corrected with a few clicks of the *Clone* tool.

If your PC struggles with Photomerge, reduce the resolution of your images a little and save the reduced images to a folder on your hard drive. Try Photomerge again with the smaller images and it should work faster.

This second example was taken with the Photomerge process more in mind, but the images were still taken hand-held. The exposure was set to manual and color balance set to sun.

An interesting idea would be to create a panorama of a member of your family, but vertically rather than horizontally. You could almost make a life-size image, but it would have to be created in the software in landscape format. The same shooting rules would apply regarding exposure and overlapping of the images.

8 Despite the shortcomings of the images, which fell well short of what you should provide for Elements to work on, the process has worked brilliantly.

For interest, you can now look at the size of the finished montage via the Menu Bar. Select *Image > Resize > **Image Size*** and you will see that the panoramas easily reach five feet in length. It is at this stage that you can apply other routine manipulations such as *Levels* and color corrections, or use *Quick Fix*.

8

Cut-outs

The question of how to do cut-outs arises frequently in digital photography, and the answer depends on a number of variables. The subject is important, but the background probably more so. You need to consider whether the tones between the subject and the background are well separated and therefore suitable for the *Magic Wand* tool. Consider what type of background it is in terms of detail and complexity. Which tool to use for cut-outs is not a straightforward question. There are a number of different *Selection* tools at your disposal in Photoshop Elements, but the ones you use most for cutting out detail and objects from one picture to insert into another are:

- **the Magic Wand**
- **the Polygonal Lasso**
- **the Lasso**
- **the Selection Brush**

You can also achieve a cut-out without a selection at all using the *Eraser* and a soft-edged brush. You can enlarge the image, change the background into a layer, and erase what you do not want. The soft-edged brush assures that you get the desired soft edge to your subject that you normally apply with the *Feather* tool.

⋀ Magic Wand

The Magic Wand *tool lets you select an area of similar colors. For example, it will select a blue sky around a subject without you having to trace around the outline. You can specify the* Tolerance *for the* Magic Wand *tool in the* Options Bar *at the top of the screen.*

In the first example, the contrast between the blue sky and the frame-filling shot of a seagull is perfect for the Magic Wand *tool.*

◁ *To cut out an object like the seagull you do not need to make any changes to the* Tolerance *setting. If you click down with the* Magic Wand *tool into the lighter blue area of the sky, a large part of that sky will be automatically selected.*

The default tolerance was not high enough to select the entire sky and Elements has recognized the difference between the darker blue and the lighter blue and has not selected it. In some cases, this might be what you want, but not here, where you need all the sky to be selected. You can increase the Tolerance value and run the tool again and Elements will select all the blue in one click.

An easier way to select the seagull is by using the Add To option from the Options Bar. This allows you to add one selection to another. Another method is to hold down the Shift key; it took just three clicks to select the entire sky.

After adding a pixel or two of feather to the selection you can copy the seagull to any other image or remove the sky via the Cut command to make a transparency—i.e. have the subject floating on a transparent background, as shown by the checkerboard effect. Change the background into a layer before cutting out that sky or you will simply cut to the background color.

Polygonal Lasso

The Polygonal Lasso *tool is one of the best tools in Photoshop Elements for making effective cut-outs. In this example, you can see that the* Magic Wand *tool would have great difficulty in selecting the background of this image. Whatever tolerance you chose or how many times you added to the selection with the* Magic Wand, *the job would defeat you because the tone difference between the hawk and the background is just too close. That is where the* Polygonal Lasso *tool comes in.*

In theory, you could use the Freehand Lasso *tool to draw around the edge of the subject, but in practice it would not be accurate enough. The* Polygonal Lasso *gives you much greater accuracy. Although this tool only works in straight lines, you can cut out any subject, no matter what shape or how intricate it may be.*

You should use this tool with the image greatly enlarged. This allows you to place the lasso selection right on the edge of the subject and also to select around the most intricate subjects. The degree of enlargement should be as far as you can go before the image gets so large that it becomes difficult to see the edge. In this case the image was enlarged almost 400%.

Polygonal Lasso tool continued overleaf

Cut-outs continued

Polygonal Lasso tool continued

Select the Polygonal Lasso tool and click down on the edge of our subject. As you move away from that point an elastic line will stretch out with the tool. The secret is to make the selection with this tool in short steps. Every time you touch down, the selection is anchored to that spot.

These steps can be longer on straighter sections, but much shorter on curved sections.

The problems you experience with this tool are firstly moving around an image that may be enlarged 400%. After a few anchor points have been made, you will run out of image on screen. If you were to change to another tool to move to the next section, you could lose the lasso selection.

When you reach this point, hold the space bar and the cursor will change to the Hand tool. Click and drag and the Hand tool will allow you to move around the enlarged image. Release the space bar and you are back with your Polygonal Lasso and you can continue making the selection.

Using this method of selection, you can select the most difficult of subjects. The effectiveness of the Polygonal Lasso tool used in this way can be seen from the completed image. The rusty iron that the hawk is standing on was also cut out using this Polygonal Lasso tool method.

TIP

If you make a mistake, your selection may suddenly join up to the starting point long before you have completed the selection. This is not a problem: simply select the Add to a Selection icon from the Options Bar or Subtract from a Selection, whichever is appropriate.

Magnetic Lasso

This tool works in a very similar way to the Polygonal Lasso. *You should work with the image greatly enlarged and draw around the edge of your subject. It doesn't matter if you stray a little from the edge with this tool as Elements will leave anchor points and the line will snap to the edge of the subject.*

The Magnetic Lasso *tool can be a quicker option if your selection does not need to be really accurate.*

Selection Brush

The Selection Brush *tool works in a different way for the same end result. This example image is very fussy and the background and different colors would defeat the* Magic Wand *tool. Working with the image greatly enlarged you can choose the* Selection Brush *and from the drop-down menu options choose* Mask *as a mode setting.*

Select a small brush for use around the edges of the subject and a larger one for other areas and you can paint a mask over the parts of the image you wish to cut out. If you make a mistake as you apply the mask, you can switch to the Selection *mode and repair it. As you switch modes a selection will appear, but you can nudge that selection back into place with the brush. When you switch back to* Mask, *the red color returns and we can continue.*

Before long, you can have your complicated selection made, your cut-out complete and a new background added.

TIP

This task can be made easier if you hold down the Shift key and mask in straight lines using the same technique as you would for the Polygonal Lasso. *Work around the outline of the object in steps. This is probably a better option for those not so skilled at freehand drawing.*

Inserting an Object from One Shot into Another

You might hear it said that a picture is a setting for something. In other words, the image is good, but it needs something extra to bring it to life. With Elements, you can add the interest digitally; by taking objects from one photo and placing them in another, you can create a realistic but more interesting composite shot.

TIP

With the Move tool selected, you can hold down the Ctrl key and click onto any of the birds within the layered stack. Elements will automatically select the layer that the bird or object occupies. This saves you from continually having to open the Layers palette.

1 I shot this old marker light on a boat trip off the coast of Australia. It is interesting and has impact, but it needs something else to improve it. On the same trip I also shot some pictures of gannets in flight, but I could not get them all in the frame together with the old marker.

2 After applying the usual adjustments to the basic image, such as *Levels* and color corection, you need to prepare the gannets. All the images were shot against a blue sky so you can use the *Magic Wand* tool to cut them out.

3 If you click into the blue sky, the whole sky is likely to be selected in one go. Here is where we can demonstrate how good the *Magic Wand* tool can be on the right subject. Feather the edge of the selection by 1–2 pixels and from the *Menu Bar* choose *Select > **Inverse*** to make the selection active on the bird rather than the sky. Alternatively, use the shortcut Ctrl+Shift+I.

4 Use the shortcut Ctrl+C to copy the selection to the Elements clipboard. After clicking back into the original image, you can use Ctrl+V to paste the bird into that image on another layer. You can then close the original seabird image down as it will now appear in the layer stack with the original image.

5 Many images where birds are added don't look right because the scale of the bird is wrong. You can use the shortcut Ctrl+T to bring up the *Free Transform* tool from the *Menu Bar* and Photoshop places a bounding box around the subject. While holding down the Shift key, click and drag a corner toggle to resize the bird. The Shift key will keep the image in proportion and you can click the tick on the *Options Bar* when complete.

6 You can repeat the same steps with the other birds and, using the *Move* tool, you can position each one into a good composition. You can also use the *Rotate > Flip > Layer* command from the *Menu Bar* to flip the birds horizontally.

Inserting an Object from One Shot into Another continued

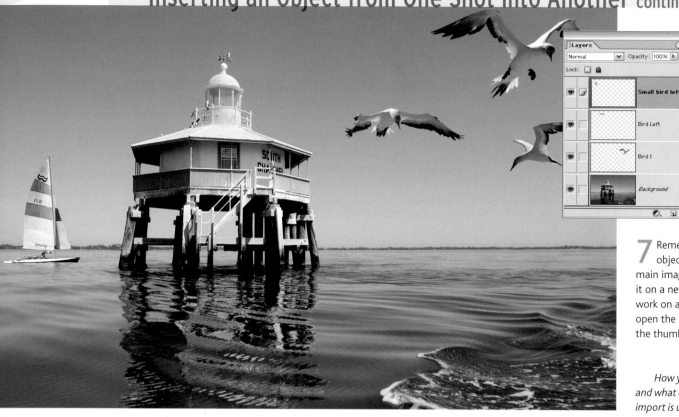

7 Remember that for each object you copy into the main image, Elements will place it on a new layer. So, before you work on any layer you must open the layers and click within the thumbnail to select it.

How you arrange the birds and what other objects you import is up to you.

The preparation of the images is exactly the same as described in steps 1 to 7 above. On this occasion, I created a border for the image (see pages 178–81) and allowed a couple of the objects to break the frame for added interest.

You can take this technique a stage further to improve your images. The basic image I took of this American bald eagle lacks impact. The bird is far too small to provide an interesting picture, so I used the continuous shooting setting on my digital camera to capture the bird in many different flight poses.

The halo effect

When you cut out objects using the *Selection* tools you can introduce an unwanted problem: the halo effect. This is caused where you remove an object from a light background and copy it into an image with a darker one. The few light pixels along the edge of the object can then be seen against the darker background. You sometimes experience the same problem in reverse with dark pixels against a light background.

All of the following techniques remove the halo effect, but your choice of method will depend on the subject.

If you look at an enlargement of one of the eagle shots against its new background, the halo can be clearly seen along the bottom of the wing and body of the bird. There are a number of ways to correct this effect.

*Once your original selection is made, but before you attempt to cut the subject out, choose Select > Modify > **Expand** from the Menu Bar. If you expand the selection by just 2–3 pixels before you add a Feather to it, you can prevent some of these pixels from causing the Halo problem. The 2–3 pixels will encroach into the subject by a small amount, but not so much that you might notice and it may leave those light pixels behind when you make your cut.*

No matter what you do, there will be certain circumstances when the halo still appears. One way to deal with it after the cut process is to select the object layer that has a halo and then select the Eraser tool. Position the object against the new background so you can see the offending pixels and enlarge the image greatly. Then choose a low Opacity from the Options Bar along with a small soft-edged brush. You can then simply erase them. Select a low opacity your work will seem gradual, delicate, and seamless.

If it is important that you do not erase pixels, you can use another technique. If, for example, you cut out an image of a boat and the mast showed a halo, by the time you removed 3–4 pixels from each side of the mast, there would be little left of the mast. To overcome this, you can select the object layer as before. Click the Lock icon within the Layers palette. This command will protect the transparent areas of the layer and prevent you from adding pixels where they are not wanted. Using the Clone tool, you can clone a few of the pixels on the inside of the halo and transfer them over the halo that is right on the edge. The Lock command prevents your work from overspilling onto the transparent part, and the halo can be removed within seconds.

In some circumstances another technique can be employed. To darken a few lighter edge pixels against a darker object like the wing of the eagle, you can use the Burn tool. If you set the options to Highlights and reduce the Exposure to a low setting, you can darken the halo to match the surroundings.

Picture in Picture

You can spend some time experimenting with the textures that come within Photoshop Elements, but you can also import and use natural textures in your images. This technique is similar to the one you would use for montage pictures, where you superimpose one or more images over another.

This example is a small rockpool. You could also use pictures of a piece of rock or slate. The technique involves taking a number of images and placing them over the stones or sections of the rock or slate.

I You need to gather the images you want to use for the project and save them to a project folder. With both the rockpool and the first image on screen, select the *Move* tool from the *Toolbar*. If you click into the image you wish to use, you can click and drag that image into the rockpool to start the layered composition.

Using the *Transform* tools, you can reduce the size and rotate the added layer so that the subject fits over the stone in the rockpool. If you then open the *Layers* palette you can reduce the *Opacity* of the layer and use the *Eraser* tool to blend the image into the stone.

2 Repeat this process for all the elements you wish to introduce into the rockpool image, saving the project after each addition. It is good practice to rename all the layers so that you can identify them easily on the *Layers* palette as you work.

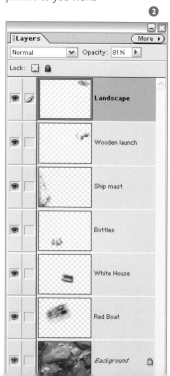

For a stronger composition, try making one of the images more prominent than the others.

In this instance, only one imported image gives all the interest needed.

3 You can use this same technique for other images. This example image of a frost-fringed piece of slate makes a perfect backdrop for the blending-in of a frosty landscape. In some cases, you can also make use of *Blend* modes such as *Hard Light* from within the *Layers* palette.

Picture-in-picture images can be fun to do. Often the images are much stronger together than they would be individually. This example makes use of some border effects for added interest.

Pattern Pictures

Some inventive pattern pictures can be produced from a simple picture taken with your digital camera and the tools of Photoshop Elements. The example featured here uses nothing more than flat shots of some autumn leaves, but using layers and the *Rotate* commands, we can still create an eyecatching image.

1 Call up the basic leaf shot and remove the background to create a transparency. The *Magic Wand* tool is good enough for this task and will easily select all the black area.

Once you have created the transparent background, you can consider sharpening the image a little and introducing some more saturation.

2 Increase the canvas size to make way for the copying of the leaf. Select *Image > Resize > Canvas Size* and increase the canvas, so that it is big enough to accommodate the growing image. You can always add to the canvas size later if you need more room.

You next need to make a copy of the leaf by dragging the thumbnail from within the layers palette down over the center copy icon at the bottom of the *Layers* palette.

3 Choose *Image > Rotate > Flip Layer Vertical* from the Menu Bar and then *Image > Rotate > Flip Layer Horizontal*. Using the *Move* tool, place the copy so that it sits like a mirror image of the original.

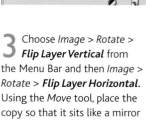

4 You can now merge the two visible layers by clicking the small black triangle icon on the tab of the *Layers* palette, which opens up a series of other layer commands. Alternatively, you can use the shortcut Shift+Ctrl+E. Don't get this *Merge Visible* command confused with *Flatten*—that will come later when the image is complete.

Copy the merged layer in the same way as you copied the first leaf and then choose *Image > Rotate > Layer 90 Right*. You can start to see how the image will be gradually built up.

5 Repeat the *Merge Visible* command so that you have four leaves on one layer. You can then copy that layer once again, but this time you need to select *Image > Rotate > **Free Rotate Layer*** and turn the second layer a little to the right by clicking and dragging outside the bounding box. Copy the layer again, which gives you three layers, and rotate the next one a little more to the right to complete the pattern.

6 Where an image like this goes from here depends on you, but I chose to introduce a second leaf and repeat the whole process to provide a centerpiece to the pattern picture. There is also nothing to prevent you from building up your pattern one leaf at a time so that every successive leaf overlaps the previous one. For this tutorial, I took a quicker route by doubling up the leaves using the *Layers* palette.

7 The pattern picture requires a good strong background, so create one using the *Gradient* tool from the *Toolbar.* Merge any remaining layers together, create a new blank layer and drag that to the bottom of the layer stack. Choose a royal blue from the *Color Picker* and hit Alt+Backspace to flood the layer with color. Blue and yellow are complementary colors, so this background will work well against the yellow leaves.

8 Elements will now allow you to draw a line anywhere on the image that defines the start and end of the gradation. Draw a line from the outer edge of the blue background inward a couple of inches and watch the result. A smooth gradation is created. You can add to that from various angles and build a pleasing gradation from royal blue to black.

Using household items
Try the same technique on everyday objects such as cutlery and you can create some very eye-catching images.

9 Choose black as the foreground color and double-click the *Gradient* tool from the *Toolbar.* Choose the *Linear Gradient* option from the *Options Bar* along with a setting of *Foreground to Transparent.*

Jigsaw

Another great effect, which is easier to create than you might imagine, is this jigsaw puzzle. This intriguing project uses nothing more than layers, layer styles, and the *Texturizer* filter, plus a little selection knowhow. Elements has many brilliant tricks that you can find if you spend some time experimenting.

> *This project needs an image without lots of fussy detail. This sunset shot, taken with a 3 megapixel camera, is perfect. The resolution of the image affects the size of the jigsaw pieces. This one, measuring 10 inches wide at 220ppi, will be fine, but an image with a higher resolution may result in the jigsaw pieces being too small.*

2 Unlike other textures where a subtle relief setting may be necessary, here you can push the relief setting higher as you want the relief to show well. You are also likely to need the *Scaling* increased to 200% or thereabouts, before clicking *OK*.

❸

4 The same texture settings give you slightly bigger jigsaw pieces.

3 If you need to increase the size of the jigsaw pieces, you need to hit the *Step Backwards* command from the *Edit* menu to remove the jigsaw texture. Go to *Image > Resize > Image Size* and add a tick into the *Resample Image* box, then reduce the *Resolution* to 150ppi and click *OK*.

To apply the jigsaw texture, go to *Textures* from the *Menu Bar*. Select *Filter > Texture > Texturizer* and, from the drop-down menu, select *Load Texture*. To find some extra textures, go to the *Presets* folder in the folder where Elements has been installed, then go into the *Textures* subfolder and select the *Puzzle* texture from the list.

TIP

As soon as the texture filter has run, you can check the size of the jigsaw pieces by viewing the image at the print size. Select the Zoom *tool from the* Toolbar *and click* Print Size *from the* Options Bar.

5 To start the process of removing some jigsaw pieces, go to the *Layers* palette via the *Palette Well* and change the background into a layer. Just double-click the layer and rename it.

6 Using the *Zoom* tool, you need to enlarge the jigsaw pieces considerably to assist you in the selection process. To make the selection of the piece(s) you can use the *Polygonal Lasso*, the *Freehand Lasso* tool, or the *Selection* brush from the *Toolbar*.

7 From the *Menu Bar* choose *Select > Feather* and add a 1 pixel *Feather* to the selection You can then cut out the jigsaw piece via *Edit > Cut* (Ctrl+X). Paste it to a new layer via *Edit > Paste* (Ctrl+V).

8 Using the *Move* tool from the *Toolbar*, you can move the piece you have cut out anywhere on the image and then repeat the cut-out steps for as many pieces as you wish to remove. If you look at the *Layers* palette, you will see each piece on a different layer.

9 You can also give your jigsaw pieces a drop shadow. This makes them appear as if they are laying on top of the image. Click the *Layer Styles* tab from the *Palette Well* and select *Drop Shadows* from the drop-down menu. Select one that you feel is appropriate and double-click it. The best option is probably the low shadow. However, once a drop shadow is applied you can open the *Layers* palette and double-click the *Layer Styles* icon to the right of the thumbnail. Another palette will then appear where you can vary the settings.

Apply the same drop shadow to each jigsaw piece and the main jigsaw layer too.

10 Use the *Transform* tools (Ctrl+T) to add a little rotation to each piece so that they do not look too regular. Position the pieces for effect, then flatten the image. This produces a white background in the space where you removed the pieces.

Borders and Frames

Borders and frames are important to the presentation of your pictures. You wouldn't put a picture on the wall in your home without a frame, because a frame presents a picture so well.

There are many ways to create borders and frames. You can use the automatic tools contained within Photoshop Elements; you can use the normal Elements tools and manually create borders and frames; or you can use some third-party border effects that you can add to Photoshop Elements. You can also use the basic border techniques to ensure that your pictures fit into a standard frame without distorting the width or the height of your picture.

0

Adding a basic border
One of the best frames to introduce to a color image is a black one, as it works well with many images where the color is dynamic and bold. Black borders also work more effectively if you add a thin white line around the outside edge of the picture before adding the frame.

1 From the *Layers* menu, change the background into a layer by renaming it. From the *Menu Bar*, choose *Select > **All*** or use the shortcut Ctrl+A. Elements will place a selection around the entire outside edge of the image.

2 With white chosen as the foreground color you can select *Edit > **Stroke*** from the *Menu Bar*. The *Stroke* palette allows you to add pixels of color to your selection line, either inside, in the center, or outside the line. The ideal *Width* setting will vary for images of different resolutions.

2

3 Add about 3 pixels to the inside of the line and click *OK* and Elements will apply a thin line. If you evaluate the image at the print size, you will be sure of getting the line thickness right. If the line is too thick, you can use the *Undo History* palette and apply it again with fewer pixels.

Go to the *Menu Bar* and select *Image > Resize > **Canvas Size*** and stipulate the width that you require your border to be. It is at this stage that you can add the size you need to fit a standard frame.

3

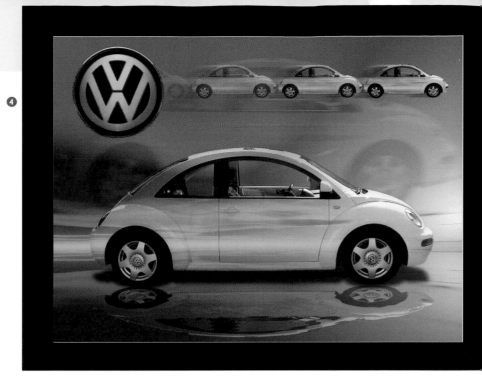

❹

TIP

If you are creating a white border for a particular frame size, add a thin stroked line to the outer edge of the border so that you have a guide to where to cut after printing.

4 From within the *Layers* palette create a new blank layer and drag that layer to the bottom of the layered stack. Flood the layer with black for a simple yet powerful result. Use a new blank layer so that you can, if you wish, experiment with other background colors by flooding the background layer with color.

Matte effect

With an image that requires a white border you can also create a matte effect, i.e. the appearance that the image is below the frame. After renaming the background and increasing the canvas size, you need to select the *Magic Wand* tool from the *Toolbar*.

You can reverse the colors and use this process for an image that could benefit from a white border along with a thin black line.

1 Click down in the transparent border area and Elements will select the area for you.
Create a new blank layer above the image and flood the selection shape with black. Create another blank layer above that and flood that with white and remove the selection via Ctrl+D.

2 Select the black layer and from the *Filter* menu add a degree of *Gaussian Blur* and the border will then appear as though it is above the image.

Borders and Frames continued

Color frames

Your image will often benefit from a color frame. If you select sample tones from within the image for the border color, the result can be very pleasing to the eye. While a contrasting hue can work well in some contexts, using colors that match those of the image makes a more complementary frame for your photo.

Borders and frames

Elements supplies some edge effects and frames for your use in the *Effects* palette found in the *Palette Well*. Click the tab and double-click the border or effect of your choice. Some of the designs verge on the tacky, and in nearly every case subtlety pays off, so try to avoid frames that might overpower your image.

You need to change the background into a layer, add your chosen canvas size, create a new blank layer, and drag that layer to the bottom of the layer stack as before. If you select the Eye Dropper tool from the Toolbar, you can sample one of the tones from within the picture and apply it to the frame.

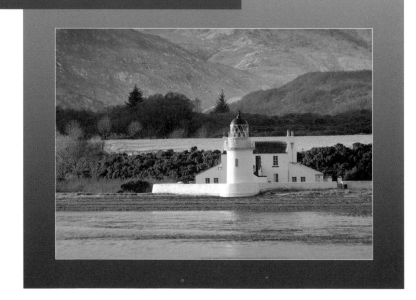

You can sample two tones of blue from the picture and apply those to the blank layer via the Gradient tool. You can also add a few pixels of monochrome Noise, which gives an attractive subtle texture to your borders.

Third-party frames and borders

There are filter, edge, and frame effects that can be purchased to work within Photoshop Elements. Some of these provide you with a remarkable selection of effects. The software is installed into the plug-ins directory of Elements and will then show in your *Filter* menu when Elements is next launched.

An example of such software is Dreamsuite Photographic Edges, which gives you not only hundreds of borders of all shapes and types, but also frames, montages, and vignettes, all at the touch of a button.

Frame Spilling Effects

OVERSPILLING

MASKS

DISTORTION

MOVEMENT BLUR

TRANSFORM TOOLS

With Photoshop Elements and a little time you can create some pretty experimental images. With this picture of the London Eye, I wanted to produce a striking picture that was different from the thousands of other images already taken of this subject.

I decided to transform a London Eye capsule into a time "spacecraft" using Photoshop Elements and to make it look as if it were bursting from out of the picture frame.

TIP

If you make a mistake and overspill the edge of the mask, don't despair. Switch to Selection *mode from the* Options Bar *and a selection will replace the mask. Using a small brush you can now nudge the overspill selection back into shape. Click back into the* Mask *option and the opaque red reappears to continue the masking.*

1 The first task is to remove the capsule from its background. You could use the *Polygonal Lasso* tool for this job, but on this occasion let's use another of Elements *Selection* tools, the *Selection* brush from the *Toolbar*.

2 You need the image enlarged considerably to start this process. From the *Layers* palette, rename the background thumbnail, changing it into a layer. Then choose the *Selection* brush from the *Toolbar*. From the *Options Bar* at the top of the screen, select *Mask* as the *Mode* option with an *Overlay Opacity* of 50%.

3 Touch down on the inside edge of the capsule with a brush size of around 20 pixels or less. Elements will create the start of your mask and show it as an opaque red. Hold down the Shift key and move along the inside edge of the capsule and touch down again to create a mask around the entire edge of the capsule. Working in small stages may help the masking process. However, if you are adept at using a freehand brush, the mask can be made this way too.

4 Once you are happy with the mask, you can switch to *Selection* mode. At present the selection contains the capsule. You need to inverse the selection in order to remove the sky. Use the shortcut Ctrl+Shft+I for the inverse command, then add a 1–2 pixel *Feather* to the selection.

Hit the Ctrl+X keys and the capsule will be free of all the background clutter and floating on a transparent background.

5 You can also cut out some of the windows in the capsule, so that when you introduce it to a new background, it will show through the windows. Use the *Selection* brush or the *Polygonal Lasso* tool to select and remove the appropriate areas so that the checkerboard pattern shows through.

6 You now need to open the image that will form your background clouds and, with the *Move* tool selected, drag and drop the capsule image into the sky. As you will see, the capsule is somewhat big for the new background and needs resizing, turning, and repositioning. Before you do that you need to create some extra space around the edge of the sky.

FRAME SPILLING EFFECTS

Frames Spilling Effects continued

OVERSPILLING

MASKS

DISTORTION

MOTION BLUR

TRANSFORM TOOLS

7 From within the *Layers* palette double-click the cloud thumbnail and rename it. Then go to *Image > Resize > **Canvas Size*** from the *Menu Bar* and add a few inches to the width and height—you can always crop back later if you add too much.

You can then select the capsule layer from the *Layers* palette and the *Transform* tools via the shortcut Ctrl+T. With this one tool you can click inside the bounding box and move the capsule around the picture space. You can click and drag outside the box to rotate the capsule and click and drag a corner toggle to size the capsule. This one tool allows you to adjust the capsule size, give it a tilt, and position it.

8 You can create a feeling of movement by first making a duplicate layer of the capsule from the *Layer* menu. If you then select *Image > Transform > **Distort***, you can create a tapering shape by dragging the toggles at the edges of the bounding box.

9 Apply *Motion Blur* from the *Filter* menu to create the streaking effect. Use the *Eraser* tool to remove some of the blurred layer so that it blends with the capsule.

IO For the border, you need to create a new layer from the *Layers* menu, drag that layer down to the bottom of the layered stack, and flood it with black.

To create the cloud spilling out of the smashed frame you need yet another new blank layer. Select the *Clone* tool and clone some clouds to it using the *Use all Layers* option from the *Clone* options. Turn off the other layers first, leaving only the sky and the new layer, or they will be cloned as well.

Take the basic idea and techniques used to make this image and add your own touches to the final result. Have fun and don't show your picture to anyone about to take a ride on the London Eye—you might make them nervous!

real world
projects

Working and experimenting with your images is always fun, but the real satisfaction of mastering Photoshop Elements comes when you share your finished efforts with others. While photography might be going digital, there is nothing to beat a high-quality print when it comes to showing off your latest masterpiece. Getting the best from a standard home printer isn't as simple as you might hope, but the tutorials on the following pages will show you how. We also won't forget the Internet or e-mail as a way of making your pictures available to others, either. Get your pictures off your computer, and out into the real world.

Printing

Printing can cause a lot of frustrations for digital photographers, but it can be our impatience that causes most of the problems in the first place.

For example, have you ever printed a landscape image in a portrait format and not realized it until a sheet of paper and a fair amount of ink have been wasted?

Once you have completed an image and are ready to print, your first thought should be, what size do I want to print the image and do I need to add a border first?

TIP

Try not to get bogged down in the resolution issue when printing. Print at the highest resolution you can. A shot from a 3 megapixel camera will have a resolution of about 200 ppi at 10 x 8 inches, and that will be adequate for a good quality Letter-sized print. You could even stretch the image to double that size as long as the print was not going to be viewed close up. Equally, printing an image at 400dpi won't affect it at all.

The most common size for printing will be 10 by 8 inches, which is a perfect size to fit on a Letter-sized sheet of paper. The modern print utility software that comes with printers can now do much of this for us, but let's deal with it manually using an example picture taken by a 6 megapixel camera.

With the image on screen, open the *Image Size* palette from the *Menu Bar*. You will see from the palette that the image from the camera is 42 by 28 inches at 72ppi. Obviously, the size is too big and the resolution too small for a Letter-sized print.

You need to resize the image so that its *Height* goes down from 42 to 10 inches. If you tick the *Constrain Proportions* box you can adjust the *Height* and the *Width* will remain in proportion. Most importantly, do not tick the *Resample Image* box. If you do, the printer software throws away pixels during the size reduction, which loses you some of the quality needed for printing.

2 Untick the *Resample Image* box and adjust the *Height* to 10 inches. As you click *OK*, nothing will seem to happen. You have to open the *Image Size* palette again to see the results of the operation.

You now have your 10-inch size and the resolution is a healthy 307ppi. From that resolution you will get an extremely good-quality image from the printer.

If you were printing the image for a 10 by 8 inch frame you can see that the 10 by 6.6 inch image is not going to fit that well—there will be a gap down the sides. One solution is to crop the image to 10 by 8 inches if there is room to do so and if cropping would not affect the appeal of the image.

Alternatively, you can reduce the print size a little more and give the image a 10 by 8 border (*see pages 178–81*).

3 You need to consider your paper choice at this stage as high-quality color photographic images need to be printed on the correct paper. This paper will generally be a heavyweight glossy, although some filtered images often look better on matte paper. Whatever paper you choose, it must be photo-quality paper or the resulting image will not display anywhere near the quality that your printer is capable of.

More prints are spoiled by rushing through your printer software options than for any other reason, so it pays to take some care here.

You will also need to specify landscape or portrait format. It is quite common to receive a warning from your printer software that the image is larger than the paper's printable area. This is due to the fact that you are printing in landscape or portrait format but you have not yet changed the format in the printer options. The software tells you that you cannot get a portrait image on landscape format paper, but you can click past this warning. Just load your paper and print your image.

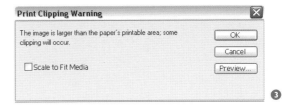

It is in the properties of the printer software that you can select your format and paper size – i.e. A4 (Letter-sized).

It is also in the properties that you are likely to be able to select paper type, such as Premium Glossy Photo Paper.

Multiple Images per Page

One of the most common questions I am asked is how to print more than one picture on a page. Photoshop Elements makes this task quite simple.

There are two reasons for placing more than one image on a page for printing. Probably the most common is to print a batch of prints to make the most economical use of paper. Four pictures on a page can be cut out into handy-sized prints to carry around in your wallet.

The other reason may be to display a small panel of images, perhaps in a frame on a wall.

I Open up the first picture of the batch of images you want to print out, then go up to the *Menu Bar* and select *File > Print > Layout > Picture Package*. Using the image used to demonstrate printing on pages 188–89, you can see that Elements has decided that you require two copies of this image and has placed them side-by-side on a 10 by 8 inch page.

From the drop-down menu titled *Layout*, you can see that you have many other choices of print layout. If you click the 4(4*5) choice Elements will place your four images onto one sheet.

Printing four images that are all the same has its uses, as when all the family want the same picture of a new baby or a wedding, but how do you get four different images on a page?

2 If you move the cursor over any of the four images that are showing on the right of the *Picture Package* palette you will see the message *Click to Select a Custom File*. When you click, a browser appears on screen and you can then find the next image you want. Windows XP users can even display the images as thumbnails, making it easier to find the next image. If you double-click your second image choice, Elements will place it into your *Print Package* palette, replacing the old shot.

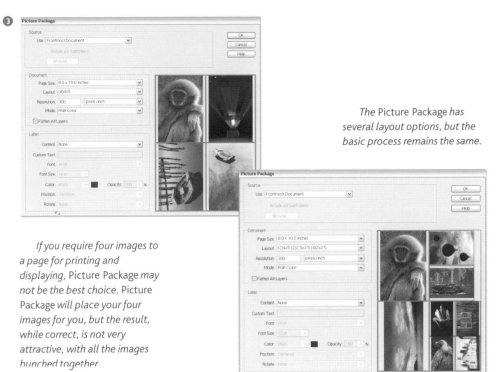

3 Click each image in turn and locate the file you want to add. It only takes seconds to have four separate pictures ready for printing. Select the paper size. For the resolution, it is a good idea to set the resolution that matches your images. That was about 200ppi for a 3 megapixel camera and 300ppi for a 6 megapixel camera.

The Picture Package *has several layout options, but the basic process remains the same.*

If you require four images to a page for printing and displaying, Picture Package *may not be the best choice.* Picture Package *will place your four images for you, but the result, while correct, is not very attractive, with all the images bunched together.*

*To create the same result manually, assuming that you require 4(4*5) images, you must prepare those images first and resize them so that you can fit four images on a Letter-sized sheet, bearing in mind that you want to retain the resolution. Make sure that the* Resample Image *box remains unticked in the* Image Size *palette—you need to retain a resolution of at least 200–300ppi for each image.*

You can then drag the images into a layered stack and increase the Canvas Size *to 10*8. Selecting each image layer in turn, position each of the images in the panel. You can display them far better as a panel with the addition of a background and a drop shadow.*

Contact Sheets

A contact sheet is a term used in film photography where negatives, usually in strips of six, are placed directly onto photographic paper and exposed to light. The developed 8 by 10 inch print is used to evaluate and aid selection of any of the 36 negatives from a roll of film.

You can create contact sheets using Photoshop Elements, but why should you wish to? You have the ability to scroll through your images using the browser within Elements. Windows XP users can see their images as thumbnails in Windows Explorer, so why make a print too?

The reason is that, after a very short while, you will not be able to store all the images you shoot on your computer —there is just not enough hard drive space. In any case, it is safer to have your images saved to CD as well as stored on your hard disk. It is not until you begin searching for that one special image that is buried somewhere on one of your CDs that you will wish you had created a contact sheet for each one. It is much easier to flick through a few Letter-sized pages of thumbnail pictures to find what you are looking for than to shuffle loads of CDs in and out of the CD-ROM drive.

Of course, Elements makes the task much simpler and faster than it ever was in the developer's darkroom.

From the Menu Bar, *select* Edit > Print Layouts > **Contact Sheet**.

The Contact Sheet *palette is divided into four sections. The top section is where you locate the folder of images to be included on the contact print. Click the* Browse *button to locate the correct folder from your hard drive.*

You can choose the page size from the Document *section. The default 10 by 8 inch size works best. You also get a choice of resolution. As an aid to finding your images, a 72ppi is adequate, but if you want to increase the resolution to 200 or 300ppi, you can do so.*

In the Thumbnail *section you can choose how many images you want to appear on a page. This is also a personal choice. However, you will generally find that the default setting is about right. Any more than six rows and five columns makes your images too small for easy identification. Use fewer if you need to differentiate between images up close.*

In the final section, you can tick the box to choose your file name on the contact sheet and the type of font. Click the OK *button and Elements will do its work. If you have a large number of images in your folder this may take some time.*

ape_colour.jpg apeman.jpg apples.jpg bales2.jpg balloons.jpg

baptism of fire.jpg Barrier reef.jpg bear.jpg Beetle.jpg Bertie Basset ge...

Biggin Hill 2002.j... bike.jpg Black country (3... Blue mountains.j... boats.jpg

burners.jpg busker.jpg cat2.jpg checking for sha... colour wheel.jpg

Copy of fig18.jpg Copy of fruit.jpg Cutout.jpg dirty glass and r... Dunstable Seren...

eagle eye.jpg hong kong.jpg iggy.jpg IMG_3250.jpg inside out.jpg

Elements does not change your original files, so you need have no concern for your original full-resolution images. Elements will copy each image, resize it and place it onto a separate page in the layout that you specified.

You can add a CD reference to your contact sheet either in Elements or with a pen after printing and you will have a permanent record of what is on each CD.

TIP

If you carry out this task for all your images, you will be sure to find it useful at some stage. Electronic catalogs have their place, but nothing beats flicking through a contact sheet.

Elements creates your contact sheet on a new blank layer. If you open the Layers palette, you can see that the background and thumbnails are both contained on separate layers. If you create your sheet on a canvas set up at about 4.5 inches square, you can add the thumbnails to a CD cover by dragging and dropping them from the Layers palette.

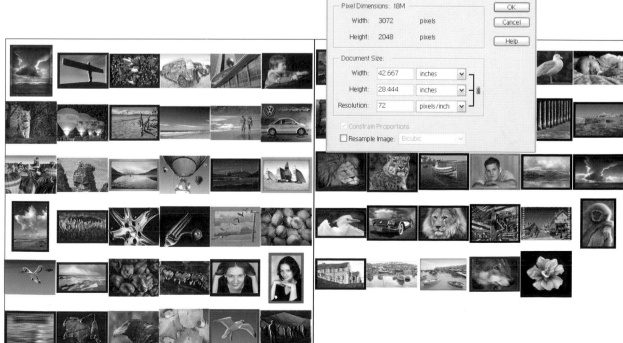

CD Covers and Inserts

There is dedicated software available for creating CD covers and inserts, but it gives you much more sense of accomplishment if you create your own using Elements. There are two types of jewel cases used for CDs: the standard type, and the slimline cases that seem to be standard for cheap CD-R discs.

1 To create a slimline jewel case insert, the first task is to create a template. You can create a single-page insert or a double-page insert that will need to be folded after printing. After selecting *File > **New***, create a square template with a width and height of 12cm (4.5 inches). This is the exact size of a slimline jewel case and will be perfect for a single-sheet insert.

2 From the *Menu Bar*, choose *Select > **All*** and then apply a thin black or gray line via the *Stroke* command from the *Menu Bar* to form your cut line. When you print your cover onto white paper, these lines will show you where to cut.

If you want a double-page insert so that you have information on the outside and inside of the cover, you need to double the size of the template. You will still need to know where the edge lines are, but also the center line of the cover. After printing you will need to know where to cut and also where to fold the cover. It is probably easier to duplicate the square with the lined edge that you have already created than create a new template.

3 To create the other side of the jewel case insert, you need to ensure that white is selected as the background color. From the *Menu Bar*, select *Canvas Size* and double the width while anchoring the template to the left.

4 Choose the *Select All* command once again, apply the stroke line around both sides of the cover, and you will have a perfect template for the jewel case.

Save this template somewhere safe on your computer for future use.

The design of your cover is a personal one, but you might find it interesting to use your own images. This can be purely for decoration or to indicate what the CD contains.

5 Open an image and with the *Move* tool selected, drag the image onto the cover template. You can use the *Transform* tools to size and rotate the images to fit in with the design and shapes. Each part of the cover can be dragged and dropped onto the layered stack and you can gradually build it up. Design both sides separately and leave room to add a title, text and any contact details that you might need.

❶

❸

❺

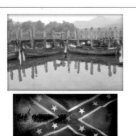

6 Add text and then use the various text options and layer styles to give it impact. Drop shadows and bevels seem to work particularly well.

Digital Audio Visual

Images gently fading from one to the other set to beautiful music

Want to put Audio Visual slide shows together ?

The CD contains all you need to know including samples of the software, where to get it and how much it costs. Install the slide show software from the CD and buy your licence over the internet for just a few dollars. The CD contains all you need to know in a step by step form from the basics to the more advanced AV.

Sample images are already prepared to guide you through the process and royalty free music in MP3 format is i
As a super bonus the Photoshop 7 toolbar is inc
for almost every tool.

This CD should auto run when put into your CD drive.
If it fails to do so you can access the tutorials and other information via your Windows Explorer and double click the Start.htm icon.
If your browser tries to take you on line, click cancel and the CD will open. Alternatively copy the entire file structure to your hard drive for ease of use. These files can be deleted at any time and nothing is written to your computer.

To run the video tutorials you will need to install a small Codec file called tscc found in the goodies/software folder on the CD.

For a logical approach to following this CD click the Introduction button from the main menu and follow the next buttons on each page. Alternatively you can move through the CD by clicking buttons on the main menu from left to right .

Digital Audio Visual

All the words and images on this CD are copyright and your use of the images contained on the CD is limited to following these tutorials. The words, pictures or parts of the pictures may not be reproduced without the permission of the author.

Your CD covers can be an extension of your creativity or they may need to be simpler in design and more instructional, especially if the CD cover is designed for a tutorial CD. In this case most of the area is taken up with text explaining how to run and use the CD.

Use Elements' ability to create a contact sheet, and you can transfer your finished contact sheet onto your CD covers. This cataloging method works especially well when you back up your collection to CD.

ape_colour.jpg	apeman.jpg	apples.jpg	bales2.jpg	balloons.jpg
baptism of fire.jpg	Barrier reef.jpg	bear.jpg	Beetle.jpg	Bertie Basset ge...
Biggin Hill 2002.j...	bike.jpg	Black country (3...	Blue mountains.j...	boats.jpg
burners.jpg	busker.jpg	cat2.jpg	checking for sha...	colour wheel.jpg
Copy of fig18.jpg	Copy of fruit.jpg	Cutout.jpg	dirty glass and r...	Dunstable Seren...

Finished Images
March 2003

kingfisher.jpg	linx.jpg	little red roster.jpg	loch.jpg	loch Awe.jpg
maltese colour.jpg	meerkat.jpg	my new car.jpg	prehistoric.jpg	ready and waitin...
salt pans.jpg	Snow leopard.jpg	the record.jpg	usa.jpg	wolf stare.jpg

Slideshows

One of the nicest ways to show your pictures to family and friends is with a slideshow; a preselected sequence of your best images put together like an automated book. With the help of Photoshop Elements, you can have a slideshow up and running within a couple of minutes with no additions to your software.

Before you start, there are a few things that you need to consider. While not essential, it looks better if you arrange all your images in either landscape or portrait format. Images that constantly change from one format to another will reduce the appeal of the slideshow.

If you can arrange your images in thematic groups such as your vacation images, or shots from an airshow you visited, the slideshow will be the better for it. You also need to consider the length of the slideshow. The most successful slideshows are rarely made by the images included; the most important aspect is what you discard. If you edit your images robustly and keep your slide shows to between three and five minutes, your viewers will always be happy to watch your shows.

From the *Menu Bar*, select *File > Automation Tools > **PDF Slideshow***. Elements will bring up the *PDF Slideshow* palette. Hit the *Browse* button and browse through your folders for the images you have prepared for the slideshow.

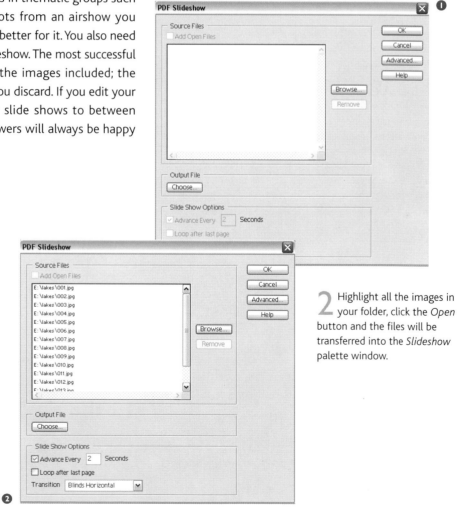

Highlight all the images in your folder, click the *Open* button and the files will be transferred into the *Slideshow* palette window.

❸

Adobe Photoshop Elements

PDF slideshow was successful.

OK

3 You can choose a transition effect from the choices in the drop-down menu and, on this same palette, how many seconds each slide remains on screen. All you have to do now is to hit the *Choose* button and decide where you want Elements to create your slideshow.

Hit the *OK* button on the *Slideshow* palette and Elements' engine room goes to work on that task for you. It may take a little while, depending on the resolution of the images you are using. When Elements is complete it will tell you so by saying *PDF slideshow was successful*.

Click *OK* and then browse for your new PDF file and double-click the *PDF* icon. Sit back and watch your slideshow fill the screen.

E-mailing Pictures

This is an area that often causes confusion and frustration, mostly because images being sent over the internet are far too large. This is particularly annoying to those on the receiving end of a huge file, bearing in mind the time it takes to download via a 56K modem.

But help is here in the form of Photoshop Elements. Before attaching an image to an e-mail, your images need to be reduced in size so that they are small enough to send quickly, but large enough to be viewed by the recipient at a good size and at a reasonable quality.

Automatic e-mail

1 The example is saved as a Photoshop file and is 18 megabytes in size. You would not be thanked for sending that image via e-mail to a friend.

2 From the *Menu Bar* select *File > **Attach to e-mail*** or use the shortcut icon just below the menu titles at the top of the screen. Elements immediately throws up a warning panel telling you that the file you are about to send may be too large for some recipients and offers to reduce the size for you.

Elements also allows you to override that warning, as on some occasions you may need to send larger images.

Manual e-mail

If you wish to prepare your image manually for attaching to an e-mail, you will need the image on screen. From the Menu Bar, *select* Image > Resize > **Image Size** *and Elements will open the* Image Size *palette.*

3 If you click *Auto Convert,* Elements not only adjusts the picture size for you, but opens your e-mail software and attaches the image to a blank e-mail. All you have to do is address the e-mail, type the message, and send it. Elements has reduced the size of the image and applied it to your e-mail as a JPEG. The size of the file is now a mere 105KB.

Elements has not reduced the size of your original saved image, so you don't have to worry about having two copies of the image on your computer.

If you open the image Elements has prepared for you by clicking the thumbnail on your e-mail, you will see that it is now 8 by 5 inches at 150ppi. The original was 42 by 28 inches at 72ppi.

I If you look at the example size, you can see that the image is 18 megabytes, which is far too big to send as an e-mail attachment. The physical size of 42 by 28 inches is also too large.

The solution is to reduce the size of the image to no more than 10 inches on its long side. Make sure that the *Resample Image* box is ticked or the size in inches will reduce but the resolution will increase, leaving the file size at 18 megabytes. With the image reduced to 10 inches on the long side, the *Resample Image* box ticked, and a resolution value at 72, you can hit *OK.*

The image will then become only 1013KB. You have removed some of the pixels that made it so big, but not so many that you affect the image quality on screen at its 10 inch size. Click the *Zoom* tool and the *Print Size* button from the *Menu* bar and you will see that the image can still be viewed very well.

However, even at 1013KB the image is still too large to send as an e-mail attachment.

2 If you save the image as a Jpeg file compressed to level 6, the 1013KB file will reduce as the format compresses the file. Choose *Save > As* from the *Menu Bar* and select *Jpeg* from the drop-down *Format* box. Select a *Quality* of 6 and hit *OK.* The image has now been saved and is a mere 48KB, which is no problem to attach to an e-mail. It is still a 10 by 6 inch image and the recipient will be able to view it comfortably.

Preparing Photos for the Web

SAVE FOR THE WEB

PRINT SIZE

SHARPNESS

BACKGROUND

SAVE OPTIONS

Preparing photos for use on a website means ensuring the picture is big enough for the viewer to be able to see and appreciate the image, but that the resolution and size of the image is small enough for a quick download. If your image takes ages to appear on screen, viewers may get bored of waiting and move on.

You need to strike a balance between size, quality, and speed. This is where Photoshop Elements offers some help with its *Save for Web* option. Before you save your image, you need to decide on the size at which you wish to display it.

TIP

As a rule of thumb, images for display on a website should be no larger than 72ppi and no wider that 700 pixels, which is just under 10 inches. This ensures that they will display on most computers without the need for scrolling. There is nothing worse than an image on screen that you need to scroll around in order to view everything—the appeal is immediately lost.

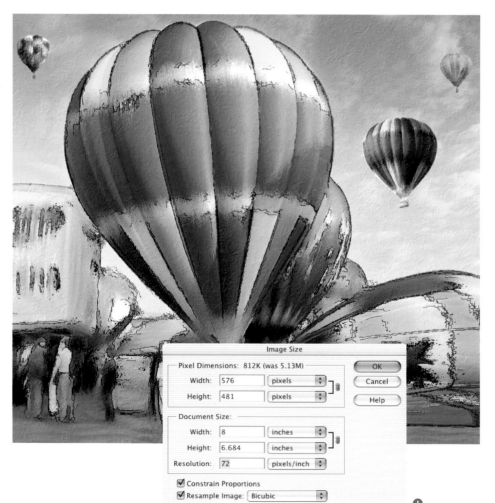

From the *Menu Bar* select *Image > Resize > **Image Size*** and reduce the size of the image for web use.

Choose an image size of no more than 8 inches on the long side unless the image is in a letterbox format, in which case you can extend the width to 9 inches. Make sure that the *Resample Image* box is ticked.

As a final test of your image size, select the *Zoom* tool and click the *Print Size* button from the options. This is the actual size that your image will appear when viewed on screen.

Unsharp Mask

OK
Cancel
☑ Preview

100%

ount: 200 %

adius: .3 pixels

hold: 0 levels

2 The first step involves reducing the size of the image, but also taking out pixels or resolution to make the image suitable for web use. This can sometimes affect the sharpness of the image.

The smaller-sized image may look OK, but if it appears to have lost sharpness you may need to replace it. Select *Filters > Sharpen > **Unsharp Mask*** from the *Menu Bar*. Add the smallest amount of sharpness until you see an improvement. Click the *Preview* button on and off to compare the before-and-after effects. This will help you ❷ to evaluate your settings.

3 You also need to consider what sort of background your image will be placed against. It could be a plain or textured background, light or dark in color. You may also want to add a thin line around the outside edge of the image so that it is presented well.

To do this, use the shortcut keys of Ctrl+A for *Select All* and a selection will appear around the outer edge of the image. From the *Menu Bar*, we can select *Edit > Stroke* and add a 2 pixel white line to the image.

The image looks very strong presented against the dark, textured background.

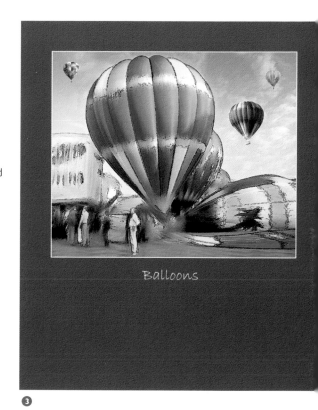

Balloons

❸

❹

Save For Web

OK
Cancel
Help

ings.

Settings: JPEG Medium
JPEG ☑ Optimized
Medium Quality: 30
☐ Progressive
☐ ICC Profile Matte:

Image Size
Original Size
Width 576 pixels
Height 481 pixels

New Size
Width: 576 pixels
Height: 481 pixels
Percent: 100
☑ Constrain Proportions
Apply

Animation
☐ Loop Frame Delay: 0.2

1 of 1 ◁◁ ◁| |▷ ▷▷

2K
o @ 56.6Kbps

30 quality

Preview In:

4 To save the file, choose *File > **Save for Web*** and the *Save for Web* palette will appear. From the options on the right-hand side you can set up the palette to save the file in JPEG format. If you click the *Quality* slider you can adjust the amount of compression you give your JPEG image.

Using the before-and-after previews on screen, reduce the *Quality* slider as far as you can before it affects the image quality to an unacceptable level. You can see that the original 812KB image will save at quality 30 to a JPEG file size of 64KB, which will take 12 seconds to download on a 56K modem.

The *Save for Web* option allows you to keep your images as small as possible, but with the advantage of being able to see how much you are affecting the image quality. The lower the JPEG compression setting, the lower the quality.

Click *OK* from the *Save for Web* palette and save the image to the place of your choice.

Web Galleries

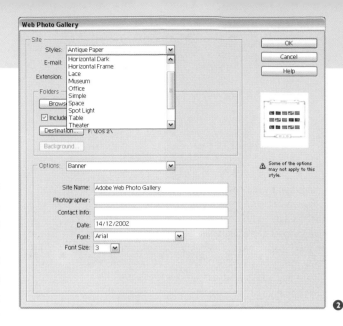

❷

Photoshop spoils you for choice when it comes to putting your images on display via your own website. You can use the *Create Web Photo Gallery* command to automatically generate a web photo gallery from your images. A web photo gallery contains a home page with thumbnails of your images and also gallery pages containing larger images. Each page contains links that allow viewers to find their way around your site. For example, when a visitor clicks a thumbnail image on the home page, a gallery page with the associated larger image will load automatically.

From the *Menu Bar*, select *File > Create Web Photo Gallery* and the *Web Photo Gallery* options will appear. The *Web Photo Gallery* palette is split into three main sections.

2 The top section of the palette is where you can decide on the style you want for your web gallery. As you select each style from the drop-down menu, Elements displays a thumbnail of what that chosen style will look like.

If you enter your e-mail address in the *E-mail Box* section, Elements provides a contact link to that address on the main thumbnail page when the gallery is created. This allows your website visitors to contact you easily.

The third choice is whether to go with an .HTML file extension or .HTM. If you create a gallery using .HTML and it does not appear to work when you load it up to your web space, try using the .HTM extension option instead.

The second section of the palette is where you tell Elements where your image folder is located and where you want the web pages to be created. Your original images will not be changed, as copies will be produced automatically by Elements. Elements will also reduce the size of your images at the same time.

❶

❸

3 In the last section of the palette, you can select your banners and enter the contact details that will appear on your main page. From the drop-down menu you can control your large image sizes and the save quality. There are similar options for the smaller thumbnails, as well as some color options to choose from. Make your preferences clear, click *OK* and Elements will do the rest for you.

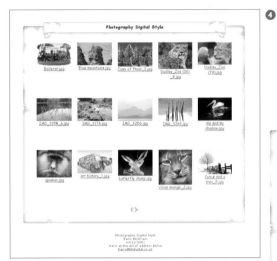

4 When the process has run, Elements will present your fully functional gallery on screen. Click on a thumbnail and the larger image should jump into view.

The page is working just as your viewers will see it on their computers. Click your e-mail contact and your e-mail program will open with an e-mail already addressed to you.

▼ *If you look at the file structure where you stored your web pages you will see that Photoshop Elements has done a perfect job*

Name ▲	Size	Type
📁 images		File Folder
📁 pages		File Folder
📁 thumbnails		File Folder
📄 index	10 KB	HTML Document
📄 index_2	7 KB	HTML Document
📄 UserSelections	1 KB	Text Document

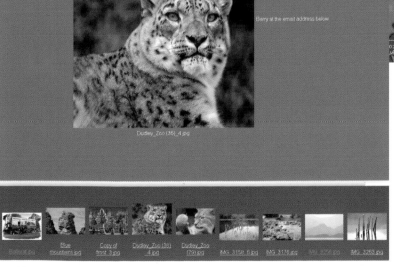

‹ ∧ *All you need to do now is to upload your files to your web space. Many internet service providers (ISPs) provide web space free of charge. Use it to create your own personal photographic gallery.*

Web Animations

Having your pictures displayed on your own website is far more fun than it may sound at first. Once you have used the tools of Photoshop Elements to create your web pages, you can then add some movement to them by creating some simple animated GIF images.

The GIF format uses 8-bit color and efficiently compresses solid areas of color while preserving sharp details in images like line art, logos, or type. It is this format that you will use to create your animated image as it is supported by most browsers.

The GIF format uses LZW compression, which is a lossless compression method. GIF files are limited to 256 colors, so saving an original 24-bit image such as our photographs as an 8-bit GIF can subtract colors from an image and reduce the quality.

Your animations must be fairly simple so that they are small in size and do not take a long time to download. You can create them in the *Layers* palette: each layer from the bottom of the *Layers* stack to the top will form a frame in your animation. These animations will be viewable in your web browser.

Follow these steps to find out how to create and optimize a simple web animation from a layered Photoshop Elements .PSD file.

1 Your animated GIF example will be based on text. From the *Menu Bar* select *File > New* and create a small panel to begin your work. Something 2–3 inches in length will be big enough at 72ppi.

Select the *Text* tool from the *Toolbar* and type the word "Photoshop." From the *Text Options Bar* at the top of the screen, select the *Warped Text* icon and introduce some shape to the text.

2 From within the *Layers* palette you need to make enough layer copies so that you have one for each letter of the word "Photoshop." Do that by dragging a thumbnail down over the center copy icon at the bottom of the *Layers* palette.

Starting from the bottom of the layers stack, you need to remove letters so that the word "Photoshop" builds up letter by letter from the bottom of the layer stack toward the top.

Create three other copy layers for the full word "Photoshop" that is at the top of the stack. This will provide a slight pause in your animation.

Elements

3 Create a new text layer by selecting the *Text* tool and clicking into the image. Type the word "Elements" and add some warped text effects to that word as well. Repeat the one-letter-per-layer technique that you applied to the word "Photoshop."

You should now have quite a large layer stack, which is not as complex as it might appear.

4 To complete the animation, select *File > Save for Web*. From the options select *GIF* from the *Settings* and tick the *Animate* box. In the *Animation* panel at the bottom of the *Options* palette, tick the *Loop* box so that your animation runs continuously, and adjust the frame delay. Here I set a frame delay of 0.2 seconds.

Click *OK* and save the GIF to a convenient place on your computer. Using Windows XP locate the file and right-click the *Animated GIF* icon. From the options choose *Open With Internet Explorer*. Your browser will open and your animation will run. This animated GIF can now be imported into any of your web pages. This example was just 18KB.

If you are good at drawing, you have the option to enhance your website with some more exciting animations. Even a quick surf around the internet will show you plenty of inspiring examples.

reference

Image Size and Resolution

The relationship between image-size and resolution if often misunderstood. If you're having trouble, this step-by-step tutorial should help clarify things. Above all else, it helps if you keep these two basic rules in mind:

1 For the best quality prints, retain all the pixels in your image up to 300ppi.

2 To send a picture as an e-mail attachment, dump some pixels from the image to make it smaller — not necessarily smaller in inches, but smaller in megabytes.

Open up a full-resolution image from your digital camera onto your screen and then select *Image > Resize > **Image Size*** from the *Menu Bar*.

If you look at the size of the image in the *Image Size* palette you will see that it is 43 by 28 inches at 72ppi. This is an image straight from a 6 mega pixel camera; the file size of 18 megabytes is shown at the top of the *Image Size* palette.

72ppi gives you 5184 pixels in every square inch (72 x 72 = 5184). The 43 by 28 inch picture has 1204 square inches (43 by 28 = 1204). Therefore 5184 pixels per inch by 1204 inches gives you a 6 million pixel image, give or take a few pixels.

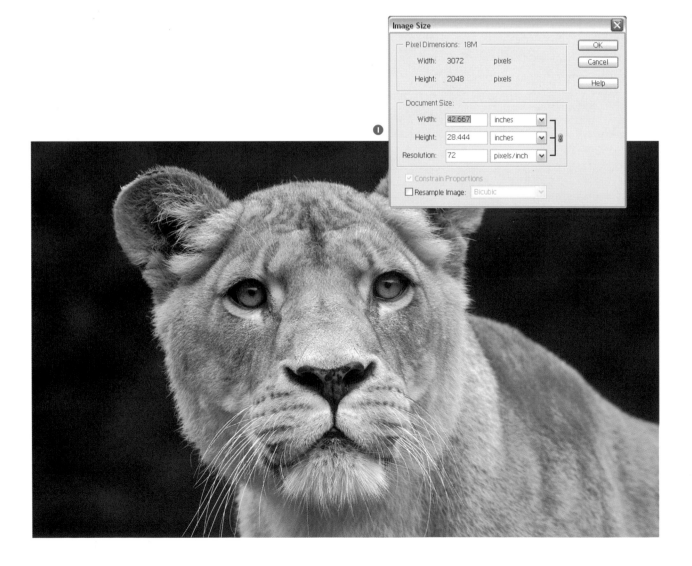

Image Size	
Pixel Dimensions: 18M	OK
Width: 3072 pixels	Cancel
Height: 2048 pixels	Help
Document Size:	
Width: 42.667 inches	
Height: 28.444 inches	
Resolution: 72 pixels/inch	
☑ Constrain Proportions	
☐ Resample Image: Bicubic	

②

2 Obviously, you cannot print a 43 by 28-inch image at home. Let's assume that you wish to print your image 10 inches on the long side to fit a Letter-sized sheet. This requires you to resize it. Open the *Image Size* palette and remove the tick from the *Resample Box*. Note the file size at the top of the *Image Size* palette—18 megabytes—and the PPI resolution (currently 72). Adjust the picture length from 43 inches to 10 inches, and the width will change automatically to just under 7 inches. Click *OK*. Nothing will appear to have happened, but open the *Image Size* palette and look again at the file size in megabytes. Although you have reduced the image dramatically, it is still 18 megabytes.

How can that be? The answer lies in the pixels per inch (ppi). In the first example, the ppi was 72. After the adjustment, it increased to 307ppi. The 6 million pixels that made up the quality in the original 43 by 28-inch image have now been compressed into 10 by 7 inches. The image won't look different on screen, but you now have a 10 by 7 inch image at 307ppi, which will give you an excellent print because every bit of detail has been retained.

④

∧ *If you select the* Zoom *tool and enlarge the image until the lioness's eye fills the screen, you see quite a different result.*

➤ *Resolution is simply how many dots you have to make up your image. The more dots, the better the image, but the more dots, the bigger the image.*

3 If you now select the *Zoom* tool and enlarge the image one click at a time until the eye fills the screen, you can still see a good-quality image, given the magnification.

③

4 Follow the same process again right from the start using the same image, but this time tick the *Resample* box. If you then compare the sizes you see a different result. The 10 by 7 inch image is now 72ppi and only 1 megabyte in size. In this example, you have discarded pixels, but as screen resolution runs at 72ppi it doesn't look much different on screen, especially at the print size.

File Formats

Photoshop Elements can save pictures in a variety of ways, but often those varieties can cause some confusion. When you see just how many formats there are, you may well ask, what do you use for the best, when do you use it, and how?

While you are working on an image, it is always a good idea to save the file as a Photoshop file with a .PSD extension. This way, you can always be sure that all the image data is saved including any layers, adjustment layers, or text layers. If you save using other formats you can lose these, along with the ability to retrieve your image later and make changes easily.

It is not until we have completed our image that the thought of saving it in another format needs to be considered. Many of the formats available are designed to enable the image to be recognized in different software packages, including web-design programs and desktop publishing software. This means many of them can be safely ignored until you find a need to save in those formats.

If you are going to save images for your own use, the three main contenders are: a Photoshop file (.PSD), a TIFF file, or a JPEG.

The JPEG format (Joint Photographic Experts Group)

This is the format you use to send an e-mail and to prepare images for web use. To save in JPEG format select *File > Save As* from the *Menu Bar* and choose *JPEG* from the drop-down format choices.

With the JPEG format, your file will be compressed and saved smaller than it would as a Photoshop or TIFF file. You are also given the choice of what level of compression to select. For e-mail and web use, a good guide is level 6, but other levels may be better with some images. You need to consider this format alongside your *Save for Web* option in Photoshop Elements.

When an image saved as a JPEG is opened it will return to its original size.

The TIFF format (Tagged-Image Format)

The TIFF format is used when you want to exchange files between different computers, as the format is supported by most paint and image-editing software. TIFF format is also what magazine editors and publishers will expect you to send them because they can be read on practically any computer, including Macs.

To save an image format as a TIFF file, select *File > Save As* from the *Menu Bar* and choose *TIFF* from the drop-down menu. You can compress them, but most TIFF files are saved without any compression.

Photoshop format

If you are storing images for your own use, the Photoshop format is fine. With this format, all the image data will be saved. The disadvantage is that file sizes can be slightly larger than some other formats, but given that modern hard drives are so big and CDs cheap, this is not generally an issue. Your images will need to be saved onto CDs at some stage anyway, no matter what file type you use.

GIF format (Graphics Interchange Format)

The GIF format reduces the colors in an image to 256, efficiently compressing solid areas of color while preserving sharp details in images like line art, logos, or type. It is this format that you use to create any animated GIFs for use on your websites. The GIF format is supported by most browsers.

EPS Format (Encapsulated PostScript)

This is used to share Photoshop files with many graphics and page layout programs.

BMP Format

This is a standard Windows image format, but it is rarely used in digital imaging circles.

TIFF

ORIGINAL

PHOTOSHOP PSD

∧ ＜ *I saved one layer image as a PSD, TIFF, and JPEG, and then compared the resulting file sizes. There is little difference between the saved TIFF and PSD files, which remained at the original 18 megabyte size. The JPEG image saved at 2 megabytes—a considerable saving, but there may be a tiny loss of quality with this compression process.*

JPEG

Color Calibration

Your monitors will display color more accurately if you make the effort to use color management and accurate ICC (International Color Consortium) profiles. Using an ICC monitor profile helps you to eliminate any color casts in your monitor. It also makes your monitor grays as neutral as possible, and standardizes image display across different monitors.

With Microsoft Windows, you can use the Adobe Gamma software that was installed with Photoshop Elements to create a monitor profile. On Mac OS, you can use the Apple calibration utility to create a monitor profile.

1 To run Adobe Gamma, go to the *Start* button and select *Settings > **Control Panel***.

2 Double-click the icon and the Gamma wizard will take you through the process.

As each panel appears, the wizard will give you clear and simple instructions to follow.

Adobe Gamma Wizard

The red, green and blue phosphors in your monitor can vary from one manufacturer to the next.

Your current monitor profile indicates that your monitor uses the following phosphors. If you know this to be incorrect, please choose a different setting.

Phosphors: HDTV (CCIR 709)

❷

< Ba

Adobe Gamma Wizard

The gamma setting of your monitor defines how bright your midtones are. Establish the current gamma by adjusting the slider until the center box fades into the patterned frame.

☑ View Single Gamma Only

Now choose the desired gamma.

Gamma: Windows Default   2.20

< Back   Next >   Cancel

Adobe Gamma Wizard

The white point of your monitor determines whether you are using a warm or cool white.

The hardware white point of your monitor is shown below. If you know this to be incorrect, choose a different setting. Or click on Measure to visually estimate it.

Hardware White Point: 6500° K (daylight)

< Ba

❷

Adobe Gamma Wizard

You can choose to work at a different white point than your monitor's hardware setting. The current adjusted white point is shown below. If desired, choose a new value.

Adjusted White Point: Same as Hardware

< Back   Next >   Cancel

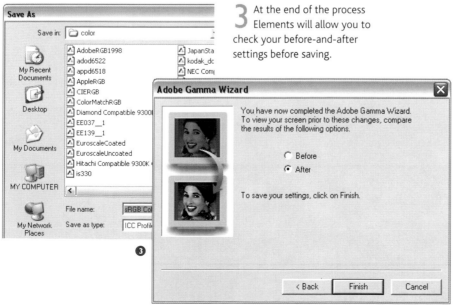

Save As

Save in: 🗀 color

My Recent Documents — AdobeRGB1998, adod6522, appd6518, AppleRGB, CIERGB, ColorMatchRGB, Diamond Compatible 9300, EE037__1, EE139__1, EuroscaleCoated, EuroscaleUncoated, Hitachi Compatible 9300K, is330 — JapanSta, kodak_dc, NEC Com

Desktop

My Documents

MY COMPUTER

My Network Places

File name: sRGB Col

Save as type: ICC Profil

❸

3 At the end of the process Elements will allow you to check your before-and-after settings before saving.

Adobe Gamma Wizard

You have now completed the Adobe Gamma Wizard. To view your screen prior to these changes, compare the results of the following options.

○ Before
◉ After

To save your settings, click on Finish.

< Back   Finish   Cancel

Further Reading and Glossary

Magazines:

The following UK and US magazines offer an excellent mix of equipment reviews, general advice on photography, and useful software tutorials:

Computer Arts
Digital Camera
Digital Photographer
Digit
PC Photo
Photoshop User
Photo Techniques
Popular Photography and Imaging

Websites:

www.bbdigital.co.uk
The author's own site, with around 50 galleries of images and many extra tutorials available online. Regularly updated.

www.davrodigital.co.uk
Another great site run by my friend, David Rowley. This popular site contains some great images, ideas, and tutorials.

www.photoshopuser.com
The site of the NAPP (National Association of Photoshop Professionals). The leading resource for Photoshop news and training, it operates for anyone - not just professional users - who is serious about image manipulation using Photoshop, though it does operate as a trade body for users.

www.photoshophalloffame.com
Photoshop Hall of Fame: a hall of fame created to recognise the people who have had a significant impact on Photoshop use, either because of the novel nature of their work or the impact of their techniques upon the development of the product.

www.creativepro.com
News, information, and resources designed for the creative professional.

www.ephotozine.com
Everything to do with photography, digital imaging, and image-editing.

www.image-resource.com
News and reviews and general help/information.

www.photoeducation.net
Education and training in photography and imaging.

www.photo.net
Major photographic resource site with useful advice, tutorials, and galleries.

Other useful links for Photography and Photoshop Elements.

Adobe
www.adobe.com

Alien Skin (Plug-ins)
www.alienskin.com

Andromeda (Plug-ins)
www.andromeda.com

Apple Computer
www.apple.com

British Journal of Photography
www.bjphoto.co.uk

Extensis
www.extensis.com

Microsoft
www.microsoft.com

Xaos Tools
www.xaostools.com

8-bit: A color mode in a digital image, where eight data bits are allocated to each pixel, producing an image of 256 grays or colors.

24-bit color: A color mode in a digital image, where 24 bits of color date are allocated to each pixel, giving a possible screen display of 16.7 million colors (a row of 24 bits can be written in 16.7 million different combinations of 0s and 1s). Eight bits is allocated to each of the three RGB color channels.

antialias/antialiasing: A technique of optically eliminating the jagged edges that appear when bitmapped images or text are reproduced on low-resolution devices such as monitors. Achieved by blending the color at the edges of the object with the background color by averaging the values of the pixels involved.

artefact: A visible flaw in an electronically prepared image, usually occurring as a result of imaging techniques. JPEG compression, for example, reduces image data by operating on square blocks of pixels, and these can become clearly visible, particularly when high contrast or color effects are applied.

aspect ratio: The ratio of the width of an image to its height, expressed as x:y. For example, the aspect ratio of an image measuring 200 x 100 pixels is 2:1.

bas-relief: An image that is embossed, so that it stands out in shallow relief from a flat background and gives an illusion of further depth.

bevel: A chamfered edge applied to an element in an image (usually type or a button) to give it a simple three-dimensional effect.

bit depth: The number of bits assigned to each pixel in an image file. Today's computer systems can handle 24-bit, or up to 16.7 million, colors. In contrast, the GIF file format can support only eight-bit color, or 256 different hues.

bitmap: A bitmap is a 'map' describing the location and binary state of 'bits' that define a complete collection of pixels or dots in an image. The term is also used to refer to pictures that have only black and white pixels.

blend mode: A feature used in Photoshop Elements and other image-editing applications to control how the pixels in one layer interact with the pixels in the layers below. This interaction could be limited to one layer covering another, but other blend modes cause more complex changes to color or brightness values.

brightness: The strength of luminescence in a pixel, going from light to dark.

burn: A method used in the conventional darkroom to darken areas of an image. Often simulated in digital image-editing packages.

calibrate, calibration: The process of adjusting a machine or piece of hardware to conform to a known scale or standard so that it performs more accurately. In graphic reproduction it is important that the various devices and materials used in the production chain – such as scanners, monitors, and printers – conform to a consistent set of measures in order to achieve true fidelity, particularly where color is concerned. Calibration of reproduction and display devices is generally carried out in software.

capture: The action of 'getting' an image, by taking a photograph or scanning an image into a computer.

CCD (Charge Coupled Device): A component used in digital imaging hardware – including digital cameras – to turn beams of light into an electrical signal that can then be converted to digital form.

clipping: Limiting an image or piece of art to within the bounds of a particular area. CMYK: Color model describing the primary colors of reflective light: cyan (C), magenta (M) and yellow (Y). Together with black (K), they are used in most forms of printing. The letter K is used rather than B to avoid confusion with blue.

clone: In image-editing applications, a retouching operation where pixels from one area of an image are copied to another area using a brush tool.

color cast: A strong color overtone that affects all or part of an image. Usually an unwanted effect, and one that can be removed by most image-editing programs.

color picker: An onscreen palette of colors in an application, from which the user can select colors to paint, draw or otherwise manipulate an image with.

composition: The effective arrangement of elements in the scene captured in the photographic frame.

compression: The technique of rearranging data so that it occupies less space on disk or transfers faster between devices or on communication lines. Different kinds of compression techniques are employed for different kinds of data – applications, for example, must not lose any data when compressed, whereas photographic images and films can tolerate a certain amount of data loss. Compression methods are described as either 'lossless' or 'lossy' accordingly.

constrain: In digital imaging, to ensure that an image maintains a particular aspect ratio or proportions during resizing or resampling.

Glossary continued

continuous tone: An image that contains infinite continuous shades between the lightest and darkest tones, as distinct from a line illustration, which has only one shade. A photographic print or slide would be an example of continuous tone, but a photo printed in a magazine would not, as its colors would have been broken down into patterns of tiny CMYK dots for the mass printing process.

contrast: The degree of difference between adjacent tones in an image from the lightest to the darkest. 'High contrast' describes an image with light highlights and dark shadows, but few shades in between, while 'low contrast' images have even tones and few dark areas or highlights.

crop: To trim or mask an image so that it fits a given area, or so that unwanted portions of the image are discarded.

cut-out: An element of an image that has been selected and seperated from the rest of the picture for purposes of composition or manipulation.

definition: The overall quality – or clarity – of an image. In a photo this is determined by the combined effects of graininess and sharpness. In a digital image resolution also has a part to play in the mix.

density: The darkness of tone or color in any image. In a transparency this refers to the amount of light which can pass through it, thus determining the darkness of shadows and the saturation of color. A printed highlight cannot be any lighter in color than the color of the paper it is printed on, while the shadows cannot be any darker than the quality and volume of ink in the printing process will allow.

density range: The maximum range of tones in an image, measured as the difference between the maximum and minimum densities (the darkest and lightest tones).

depth of field: A photographic function that defines the extent to which the area in front of the lens will appear in sharp focus. The effects of depth of field are often used for creative purposes.

desaturate: To reduce the purity of a color, thus making it grayer.

diffuser: Any material that scatters transmitted light, thus increasing the area of the light source.

digital: Anything operated by or created from information represented by binary digits. Distinct from analog, in which information is stored by a physical variable.

digital data: Information stored or transmitted as a series of 1s and 0s ('bits'). Because values are fixed (so-called discrete values), digital data is more reliable than analog data, as the latter is susceptible to uncontrollable physical variations.

digital image: Image converted to (or created in) the digital domain. Elements of the image are represented by groups of pixels, each with their own discrete color and brightness values.

dithering: A technique of 'interpolation' which calculates the average value of adjacent pixels. This technique is most often used to add extra pixels to an image – to smooth an edge, for example, or to simulate a large range of hues from a smaller selection.

dodge: A method of lightening areas in a photographic print by selective masking. Many image-editing applications can simulate the effect through digital means.

dots per inch (dpi): A unit of measurement used to represent the resolution of output devices, including printers. Also applied, erroneously, to monitors and digital images, where the resolution should be more properly be expressed in pixels per inch (ppi). The closer the dots or pixels (the more there are to each inch), the better the quality.

duotone: A monochromatic image combining two halftones with different tonal ranges made from the same original. When printed in different tones of the same original, a wider tonal range is reproduced than would be possible with a single color. Special effects can be achieved by using the same technique and printing with different colored inks.

exposure: The amount of light allowed to reach a photosensitive material, such as photographic film or a CCD imaging sensor, to enable the recording of an image. The amount of exposure has a dramatic effect on the tonal and color values of the shot. Overexposure leads to bleached colors and poor contrast. Underexposure results in dark, gloomy, and badly defined pictures.

feathering: A similar process to antialiasing, this blurs the edge pixels of a selection to give a soft border.

fill: An image-editing operation that covers a defined area with a particular color or texture.

filter: Strictly speaking, a filter can be any component in a software program that provides the basic building blocks for processing data. In image-editing and drawing applications, the term usually refers to the advanced features used to apply special effects to an image.

GIF: Graphics Interchange Format. A file format designed to produce very small, optimized image files for the Web. GIFs also provide basic inbuilt animation features. The format allows for simple transparency but can only contain up to 256 colors.

graduation / gradation: The smooth transition from one color or tone to another.

gradient: An effect or fill that uses graduation to control the color or brightness values of the affected pixels.

grain: The density of light-sensitive crystals in a photographic emulsion. Fine grain allows more detail, but the film is less light-sensitive. Coarse grain is sometimes used for a graphic effect, and this can also be simulated using digital means.

graphic: A general term describing any illustration or drawn design. Can also refer, more specifically, to 'graphic' images where the emphasis is on high-impact visuals with strong lines and dramatic tones at the expense of realism or fine detail.

grayscale: The rendering of an image in a range of grays from white to black. In a digital image and on a monitor, this usually means that an image is rendered with eight bits assigned to each pixel, giving a maximum of 256 levels of gray.

halo effect: An artefact created when a cut-out is copies to a new image or a different area of the same image. The pixels around the cut-out show up against the new background, creating the effect of a halo surrounding it.

highlight: To mark an item, such as a section of text, icon, or menu command, to indicate that it is either selected or active.

HSL: A color model based on the variables of Hue, Saturation, and Lightness.

hue: A color as found in its pure state in the spectrum.

image size: A description of the dimensions of an image. Depending on the type of image being measured, this can be in terms of linear dimensions, resolution or digital file size.

import: To bring text, pictures or any other form of data into a document.

interface: A term most often used to describe the screen design that links the user with the computer program or website. The quality of the user interface often determines how well users will be able to access and use all the features in the program, or navigate their way around the pages within the website.

interpolation: A calculation used to estimate unknown values that fall between known values. This process is used to redefine pixels in bitmap images after they have been modified in some way, such as when an image is resized or rotated, or if color corrections have been made.

JPEG (Joint Photographic Expert Group): A digital image file format used for continuous tone images such as photographs. It uses a lossy compression algorithm to squeeze large images into compact files. The Joint Photographic Expert Group first created the format.

Kelvin temperature scale (K): A unit of measurement that describes the color of a light source, beginning with absolute darkness and rising to incandescence.

landscape format: An image or page format in which the width is greater than the height. Also known as 'horizontal format'.

layer: In Photoshop Elements, a level to which you can consign an element of the design you are working on, so that you can separate it and work on it independently. Selected layers may be active (meaning you can work on them) or inactive, and can be copied, deleted, or made transparent and even invisible.

lasso: A freehand tool used in image-editing applications to select a portion of an image. In Photoshop Elements this also comes in a magnetic variety, which identifies the edges of a particular element, and a polygonal version, which creates straight-edged selections around an object.

Levels: The range of tones in an image going from the darkest to the lightest. Photoshop Elements has a Levels tool designed to give complete control over the tonal range of a digital photograph.

light table: A table or box with a translucent glass top lit from below, giving a color-balanced light suitable for viewing transparencies and, if necessary, color-matching them to proofs.

lightness: The tonal measure of a color relative to a scale running from black to white. Also called 'brightness'.

line art: Diagrams and graphics comprising (normally) black lines on a white background.

lossless / lossy: Refers to data-losing qualities of different compression methods: lossless means that no image information is lost; lossy means that some (or much) of the image data is lost in the compression process.

magic wand: In image-editing applications, a tool used to select those areas of an image which possess similar brightness or color values in order to operate on them.

marquee: An image-editing tool used to make selections based on simple rectangular or elliptical shapes.

Glossary continued

mask: Originally a material used to protect all or part of a image during photographic reproduction. In image-editing applications, a mask is used to prevent alterations from affecting the masked portion of an image.

master: An original item from which all copies are made, or upon which any changes are marked or made.

megapixel: One million pixels. A term used to describe the CCD and capture capabilities of a digital camera. A four megapixel camera takes shots of twice the resolution of a two megapixel model.

menu bar: In most applications, the bar at the top of the screen that hosts the various drop down menus used to access and control program features.

midtones / middletones: The range of tonal values in an image anywhere between the darkest and lightest – usually those approximately half-way.

moiré: An unintended pattern that frequently occurs when a photograph or page from a book or magazine is scanned. Scanner software and some image-editing applications contain filters to counter it.

monochrome: An image of varying tones reproduced using inks of a single color. While this is usually black ink on white paper, this isn't necessarily the case.

montage: A photographic technique, simulated in Photoshop Elements, where parts from two or more images are composited to create a new picture.

multimedia: A generic term used to describe any combination of sound, video, animation, graphics, and text incorporated into a software product or presentation.

opacity: In image editing, the extent to which one layer is transparent or opaque, allowing the pixels in layers below to show through.

options bar: In Photoshop Elements, the bar at the top of the screen which displays the options for the tool in current use.

palette (1): The subset of colors needed to display an image. For instance, a GIF image has a palette containing a maximum of 256 distinct colors.

palette (2): A part of the interface in many image-editing and visual-design applications, a palette is a window that contains features such as tools, measurements, options, or other functions. In most applications, palettes can be moved, hidden, and even docked together if desired.

palette well: In Photoshop Elements, an area of the screen interface where frequently used palettes

are docked. These palettes can be viewed, dragged from, or dropped on to the Palette Well as needed.

panorama: An image created from several shots of the same scene that simulates a large, wide-angle shot in a panoramic format.

perspective: A technique of rendering 3D objects on a 2D plane, duplicating the 'real world' view by creating an impression of the object's relative position and size when seen from a certain point-of-view. The perspective narrows as distance increases.

picture skew: The distortion of an image by slanting the two opposite sides of the image rectangle away from the horizontal or vertical.

pixel: Acronym for picture element. The smallest component of a digital image – a single block in the bitmap grid, with its own specific color and brightness values.

plug-in: Subsidiary software for a browser or other package that enables it to perform additional functions, e.g., play sound, films, or video.

PNG (portable network graphic): A digital image format that uses a highly sophisticated compression technique, which is said to result in file sizes typically 30 per cent smaller than those for comparable GIFs. The PNG format can also support the

full 24-bit color palette, and as a lossless format is less likely to cause artefacts than using JPEG.

polarizing filter: A popular photographic filter used to remove polarized light, including reflected light, resulting in brighter colors and richer skies.

portrait format: An image or page in a vertical format. Also called 'upright format.'

posterize/posterization: To divide, by photographic or digital means, a continuous-tone image into either a predefined or arbitrary number of flat tones. Also known as tone separation.

proprietary: A design, product, or format developed, marketed and owned by a single company or person. While some proprietary formats become standard formats, most standards are defined by some form of cross-industry organisation.

quick fix: A tool, specific to Photoshop Elements, which allows users to correct the most common faults seen in photographs.

RAM: (Random Access Memory) The memory 'space' used by the computer, into which some or all of an application's code is loaded while you work with it. Generally, the more memory, the better. Imaging software, such as Photoshop Elements, might need up to five times the amount of available RAM that an image file would normally occupy in order to process the image.

Red eye: A common problem in portrait shots where the camera's flash is reflected in the blood cells at the back of the eye, giving the pupils a fiendish red cast.

rescale: Amending the size of an image by proportionally reducing or increasing its height and width.

resolution: The degree of quality, definition or clarity with which an image is reproduced or displayed. In a photograph this would be the result of focus, clarity and grain structure. In a digital image, resolution refers directly to the numbers of pixels contined within a finite area of the image.

restore: To restore something to its original state or, in the case of a document, to its last 'saved' version. Also called 'revert.'

reticulation: An effect of photographic processing where the film emulsion adopts a distupted or crazed pattern. Usually undesirable, the effect is simulated in some image-editing programs as a quick means of aging an image artificially.

retouching: Altering an image, artwork or film to modify or remove imperfections. Can be done using mechanical methods (knives, inks and dyes) or digitally, using Photoshop or a similar image-editing program.

RGB (Red Green Blue): The primary colors of the 'additive' color model, used in video technology, computer monitors, and for graphics such as for the Web and multimedia that will not ultimately be printed by the four-color (CMYK) process.

saturation: A variation in color, affecting hues of the same brightness, ranging from none (gray) through pastel shades (low saturation) to pure (fully saturated) color.

scanning: An electronic process that converts a hard copy of an image into digital form. The scanned image can then be manipulated.

selection: A portion of an image that has been selected for manipulation. Any adjustment will only affect this chosen area.

sepia: A shade of brown, which lends its name to the sepia tone, a rich monochrome print in which shades of gray appear as shades of brown.

shadow areas: The parts of an image that are darker or denser than the majority.

soft-focus: An effect that softens or diffuses the lines of an image without altering the actual focus. Soft-focus has been used traditionally to confer a romantic feel to portraits, and can now be simulated in software.

thumbnail: A small representation of an image used mainly for identification purposes in an image listing or, within Photoshop, for illustrating layers.

tonal compression: The effects on an image, usually caused by scanning or printing, where the range of tones, from light to dark, is reduced to the detriment of the picture.

toolbar: In applications, a standard palette which ensures that the most-commonly used tools are always available at a click.

unsharp masking (USM): A traditional film-compositing technique used to 'sharpen' an image. This effect can also be achieved digitally. Most image-editing applications contain a USM filter which can enhance the details in a scanned or digital photo, and give an impression of improved clarity.

USB (Universal Serial Bus): A port (socket) for connecting peripheral devices to your computer which can be daisy-chained together. These can include devices such as scanners, printers, keyboards and hard drives.

vector: A mathematical description of a line that is defined in terms of physical dimensions and direction. Vectors are used in drawing and image-editing packages to define shapes (vector graphics) that are position- and size-independent.

vignetting: A noticeable fading at the edges of an image caused by a reduction in light levels at the edges of the frame. While a problem if caused by deficiencies in a camera, vignetting can also be used to positive effect and simulated via digital means.

virtual: Any thing that, while it doesn't exist physically, can be made to appear as if it does. For example, virtual memory is a simulation of RAM on the hard disk, which the computer uses as if it were physical RAM.

Index

cut-outs 164
day into night 91
Diffuse Glow Filter 139
Dry Brush filter 141
halo effect 171
hand tinting 121
montages 157, 158
old photographs 103
painterly effects 129
picture in picture 172
respray 143
shapes 151
sky replacement 81
soft focus 55
text 147
Expand 79, 171
Exposure 52–3, 84, 159, 171
exposure adjustment 34–5
Eye Dropper 32, 73, 76, 101, 104, 138, 180
eyes 94–5, 97
color changes 99
enhancement 92–3
lightening 41
red removal 42–3
removing soft focus 53

fading 100–1, 103
Feather 41, 59, 68, 70, 75, 111
action shots 112
adding interest 84
damaged photos 105
day into night 90
distortion 64, 66
halo effect 171
inserting objects 168
jigsaw 177
monochrome 115
montages 154
portraits 95
respray 142
sharpening 45
sky replacement 78
text 148
texture 135
tones 117
vignettes 122, 123
weather improvement 82
File Browser 20

file formats 210–11
film scanners 14, 15
Filters 9, 126–31
see also individual filters
distortion 64
First Click 42
Fit on Screen 84, 162
Flag 145
Flatten 31, 33, 39, 58, 63, 68, 81, 90, 101
damaged photos 107
jigsaw 177
monochrome 115
montages 155, 158
painterly effects 129
portraits 95
watercolor 131
Flip 110–11, 169
Flip Horizontal 26
Flip Layer Horizontal 110, 174
Flip Layer Vertical 174
Flip Vertical 27
Flow 41, 61
fluorescent light 40–1
Focus, Auto Focus 26
font 145
size 144, 145
Foreground to Background 106
Foreground to Transparent 73, 76, 83, 114, 175
Frame From Video 17
frame spilling effects 182–5
frames see borders
freckle removal 97
Free Transform 31, 66, 71, 81, 111
inserting objects 169
montages 155, 157, 158
Freehand Lasso 41, 66, 68, 75, 82, 111, 112, 115, 123, 165
Frosted Glass 134–5

gardening 48
Gaussian Blur 54–5, 58–9, 89, 90, 179
line work 152
montages 155
watercolor 131

GIF format 204, 205, 211
Glowing Edges filter 140
Grab Frame 17
Gradient 67, 73, 76–7, 83, 180
damaged photos 106
day into night 91
monochrome 114
pattern pictures 175
graduated filters 76–7
Grid 30, 31, 63

hair coloring 98–9
halo effect 79, 171
hand tinting 120–1
Hard Light 121, 157, 158, 173
Highlights 37, 52–3, 74, 81, 84–5, 171
montages 159
portraits 92, 94
histograms 32, 74, 92, 106
horizons, sloping 30–1
Horizontal Type 144
Horizontal Type Mask 148
How To tab 34, 35
Hue and Saturation 25, 38–9, 65, 80, 85, 88, 116–17, 118
ageing effects 124
monochrome 139
montages 159
painterly effects 129

Image Balance 137
Image Size 15, 111, 163, 176, 188–9, 191, 199, 200, 208–9
importing images
from cameras 12–13
from scanners 14–15
Increase Red 83
interpolation 29
Inverse 64, 112, 135, 153, 168, 183
Invert 130, 152

jigsaw 176–7
JPEG format 199, 201, 210

landscape format 188, 189
landscapes
adding interest 84–5

day into night 88–91
light improvement 86–7
retouching 74–91
sky replacement 78–81
weather improvement 82–3
Lasso 50, 134
see also Freehand Lasso; Polygonal Lasso
cut-outs 164
Magnetic Lasso 167
Layers 21
action shots 113
adding interest 85
animations 204
background 70, 72–3
borders 178–9
colored pencil filter 138
contact sheets 193
contrast 32
converging verticals 62
copying images 70–1
day into night 89–90
depth of field 58
Diffuse Glow Filter 139
distortion 65–7
Dry Brush filter 141
exposure adjustment 34
flipping 110–11
frame spilling 182–5
Glowing Edges filter 140
graduated filters 77
hair color 98–9
hand tinting 120
inserting objects 168–70
jigsaw 177
light improvement 86–7
line work 153
monochrome 114
montages 154–7
old photographs 101–2
painterly effects 126–9
pattern pictures 174–5
picture in picture 172–3
pixelation 39
portraits 94–5, 96–7
respray 142–3
shapes 151
sketch filter 137
sky replacement 78, 81

Index continued

author

Acknowledgments

First of all, thanks to Adobe, who have produced such superb software. Before Elements, many of the projects in this book would have been possible, but a lot more difficult to create and to follow.

Thanks, too, to Barry Colquhoun who encouraged me to begin writing tutorials on Photoshop in the early days of Digital Photography. Without him I may never have written anything at all, so he has a lot to answer for. I would also like to thank Barry for the use of a painterly technique that he developed and freely passed on to me for my use in part four of this book.

Most of all, a big thankyou to my wife, who tolerates the hours I spend working on images on the computer and the many hours when I had my head down creating the work for this book. Also, thanks to her, in advance, for the time I will spend on the next one.

About the author:

Barry Beckham is 53 years old and has been involved in Photography most of his adult life. His early involvement in photography came when he joined a Photographic Society and he quickly became involved in all the activities such as development and printing of both black and white and color images. Barry found a creative outlet for his photography via slideshows, and toured clubs in the UK lecturing on the subject.

Barry was introduced to a very early version of Adobe Photoshop some years ago when PCs were almost steam driven and every task took ages to complete. He saw the potential of the digital revolution and stuck with it, learning the techniques and skills required.

The author now realises that he was a digital photographer all his life, just waiting for the equipment to be invented. He now works 100% digital using a Nikon Coolpix 990 digital camera and a Canon EOS D60 digital SLR. Barry writes regularly for leading UK digital imaging magazines, and lectures to amateur and professional photographers on Photoshop and Photoshop Elements.